Apples of gold for young men and women, and a crown of glory for old men and women, or, The happiness of being good betimes and the honour of being an old disciple clearly and fully discovered (1659)

Thomas Brooks

Apples of gold for young men and women, and a crown of glory for old men and women, or, The happiness of being good betimes and the honour of being an old disciple clearly and fully discovered
Happiness of being good betimes and the honour of being an old disciple.
Brooks, Thomas, 1608-1680.
[Edition statement:] The third edition corrected.
[28], 259, [1] p.
London : Printed by R.I. for John Hancock,
Wing / B4923A
English
Reproduction of the original in the Harvard University Library

Early English Books Online (EEBO) Editions

Imagine holding history in your hands.

Now you can. Digitally preserved and previously accessible only through libraries as Early English Books Online, this rare material is now available in single print editions. Thousands of books written between 1475 and 1700 and ranging from religion to astronomy, medicine to music, can be delivered to your doorstep in individual volumes of high-quality historical reproductions.

We have been compiling these historic treasures for more than 70 years. Long before such a thing as "digital" even existed, ProQuest founder Eugene Power began the noble task of preserving the British Museum's collection on microfilm. He then sought out other rare and endangered titles, providing unparalleled access to these works and collaborating with the world's top academic institutions to make them widely available for the first time. This project furthers that original vision.

These texts have now made the full journey -- from their original printing-press versions available only in rare-book rooms to online library access to new single volumes made possible by the partnership between artifact preservation and modern printing technology. A portion of the proceeds from every book sold supports the libraries and institutions that made this collection possible, and that still work to preserve these invaluable treasures passed down through time.

This is history, traveling through time since the dawn of printing to your own personal library.

Initial Proquest EEBO Print Editions collections include:

Early Literature

This comprehensive collection begins with the famous Elizabethan Era that saw such literary giants as Chaucer, Shakespeare and Marlowe, as well as the introduction of the sonnet. Traveling through Jacobean and Restoration literature, the highlight of this series is the Pollard and Redgrave 1475-1640 selection of the rarest works from the English Renaissance.

Early Documents of World History

This collection combines early English perspectives on world history with documentation of Parliament records, royal decrees and military documents that reveal the delicate balance of Church and State in early English government. For social historians, almanacs and calendars offer insight into daily life of common citizens. This exhaustively complete series presents a thorough picture of history through the English Civil War.

Historical Almanacs

Historically, almanacs served a variety of purposes from the more practical, such as planting and harvesting crops and plotting nautical routes, to predicting the future through the movements of the stars. This collection provides a wide range of consecutive years of "almanacks" and calendars that depict a vast array of everyday life as it was several hundred years ago.

Early History of Astronomy & Space

Humankind has studied the skies for centuries, seeking to find our place in the universe. Some of the most important discoveries in the field of astronomy were made in these texts recorded by ancient stargazers, but almost as impactful were the perspectives of those who considered their discoveries to be heresy. Any independent astronomer will find this an invaluable collection of titles arguing the truth of the cosmic system.

Early History of Industry & Science

Acting as a kind of historical Wall Street, this collection of industry manuals and records explores the thriving industries of construction; textile, especially wool and linen; salt; livestock; and many more.

Early English Wit, Poetry & Satire

The power of literary device was never more in its prime than during this period of history, where a wide array of political and religious satire mocked the status quo and poetry called humankind to transcend the rigors of daily life through love, God or principle. This series comments on historical patterns of the human condition that are still visible today.

Early English Drama & Theatre

This collection needs no introduction, combining the works of some of the greatest canonical writers of all time, including many plays composed for royalty such as Queen Elizabeth I and King Edward VI. In addition, this series includes history and criticism of drama, as well as examinations of technique.

Early History of Travel & Geography

Offering a fascinating view into the perception of the world during the sixteenth and seventeenth centuries, this collection includes accounts of Columbus's discovery of the Americas and encompasses most of the Age of Discovery, during which Europeans and their descendants intensively explored and mapped the world. This series is a wealth of information from some the most groundbreaking explorers.

Early Fables & Fairy Tales

This series includes many translations, some illustrated, of some of the most well-known mythologies of today, including Aesop's Fables and English fairy tales, as well as many Greek, Latin and even Oriental parables and criticism and interpretation on the subject.

Early Documents of Language & Linguistics

The evolution of English and foreign languages is documented in these original texts studying and recording early philology from the study of a variety of languages including Greek, Latin and Chinese, as well as multilingual volumes, to current slang and obscure words. Translations from Latin, Hebrew and Aramaic, grammar treatises and even dictionaries and guides to translation make this collection rich in cultures from around the world.

Early History of the Law

With extensive collections of land tenure and business law "forms" in Great Britain, this is a comprehensive resource for all kinds of early English legal precedents from feudal to constitutional law, Jewish and Jesuit law, laws about public finance to food supply and forestry, and even "immoral conditions." An abundance of law dictionaries, philosophy and history and criticism completes this series.

Early History of Kings, Queens and Royalty

This collection includes debates on the divine right of kings, royal statutes and proclamations, and political ballads and songs as related to a number of English kings and queens, with notable concentrations on foreign rulers King Louis IX and King Louis XIV of France, and King Philip II of Spain. Writings on ancient rulers and royal tradition focus on Scottish and Roman kings, Cleopatra and the Biblical kings Nebuchadnezzar and Solomon.

Early History of Love, Marriage & Sex

Human relationships intrigued and baffled thinkers and writers well before the postmodern age of psychology and self-help. Now readers can access the insights and intricacies of Anglo-Saxon interactions in sex and love, marriage and politics, and the truth that lies somewhere in between action and thought.

Early History of Medicine, Health & Disease

This series includes fascinating studies on the human brain from as early as the 16th century, as well as early studies on the physiological effects of tobacco use. Anatomy texts, medical treatises and wound treatment are also discussed, revealing the exponential development of medical theory and practice over more than two hundred years.

Early History of Logic, Science and Math

The "hard sciences" developed exponentially during the 16th and 17th centuries, both relying upon centuries of tradition and adding to the foundation of modern application, as is evidenced by this extensive collection. This is a rich collection of practical mathematics as applied to business, carpentry and geography as well as explorations of mathematical instruments and arithmetic; logic and logicians such as Aristotle and Socrates; and a number of scientific disciplines from natural history to physics.

Early History of Military, War and Weaponry

Any professional or amateur student of war will thrill at the untold riches in this collection of war theory and practice in the early Western World. The Age of Discovery and Enlightenment was also a time of great political and religious unrest, revealed in accounts of conflicts such as the Wars of the Roses.

Early History of Food

This collection combines the commercial aspects of food handling, preservation and supply to the more specific aspects of canning and preserving, meat carving, brewing beer and even candy-making with fruits and flowers, with a large resource of cookery and recipe books. Not to be forgotten is a "the great eater of Kent," a study in food habits.

Early History of Religion

From the beginning of recorded history we have looked to the heavens for inspiration and guidance. In these early religious documents, sermons, and pamphlets, we see the spiritual impact on the lives of both royalty and the commoner. We also get insights into a clergy that was growing ever more powerful as a political force. This is one of the world's largest collections of religious works of this type, revealing much about our interpretation of the modern church and spirituality.

Early Social Customs

Social customs, human interaction and leisure are the driving force of any culture. These unique and quirky works give us a glimpse of interesting aspects of day-to-day life as it existed in an earlier time. With books on games, sports, traditions, festivals, and hobbies it is one of the most fascinating collections in the series.

The BiblioLife Network

This project was made possible in part by the BiblioLife Network (BLN), a project aimed at addressing some of the huge challenges facing book preservationists around the world. The BLN includes libraries, library networks, archives, subject matter experts, online communities and library service providers. We believe every book ever published should be available as a high-quality print reproduction; printed on-demand anywhere in the world. This insures the ongoing accessibility of the content and helps generate sustainable revenue for the libraries and organizations that work to preserve these important materials.

The following book is in the "public domain" and represents an authentic reproduction of the text as printed by the original publisher. While we have attempted to accurately maintain the integrity of the original work, there are sometimes problems with the original work or the micro-film from which the books were digitized. This can result in minor errors in reproduction. Possible imperfections include missing and blurred pages, poor pictures, markings and other reproduction issues beyond our control. Because this work is culturally important, we have made it available as part of our commitment to protecting, preserving, and promoting the world's literature.

GUIDE TO FOLD-OUTS MAPS and OVERSIZED IMAGES

The book you are reading was digitized from microfilm captured over the past thirty to forty years. Years after the creation of the original microfilm, the book was converted to digital files and made available in an online database.

In an online database, page images do not need to conform to the size restrictions found in a printed book. When converting these images back into a printed bound book, the page sizes are standardized in ways that maintain the detail of the original. For large images, such as fold-out maps, the original page image is split into two or more pages

Guidelines used to determine how to split the page image follows:

- Some images are split vertically; large images require vertical and horizontal splits.
- For horizontal splits, the content is split left to right.
- For vertical splits, the content is split from top to bottom.
- For both vertical and horizontal splits, the image is processed from top left to bottom right.

Mr. BROOKS his Apples of Gold.

Apples of Gold

FOR
Young Men and Women,
AND,
A CROWN of GLORY for Old Men and Women:

OR,

The Happiness of being Good betimes,
And the Honour of being an Old Disciple.

Clearly and fully discovered, and closely and faithfully applied.

ALSO,

The Young Mans Objections answered.
And the Old Mans Doubts resolved.

By THOMAS BROOKS Preacher of the Gospel at Margarets New Fishstreet-hill.

The Third Edition corrected.

But I thy Servant fear the Lord from my youth, 1 Kings 18. 12.

The hoary head is a Crown of Glory, if it bee found in a way of Righteousness, Prov. 16. 31.

London, Printed by R. I. for *John Hancock*, to be sold at the first Shop in *Popes-head-Alley*, next to *Cornhill*, near the Exchange. 1659.

OFFICE LIBRARY
GIFT OF THE
MISSOURI HISTORICAL SOCIETY

To all Young Persons throughout the Nations, especially those (of both Sexes) who begin to turn their faces towards *Zion*.

Dear Hearts,

A Word spoken in due season, how good is it? it is often like Apples of Gold in Pictures of Silver; many times such a word is sweet, precious, pleasing, delectable, and strong in its operation. A company of near friends dining together one Sabbath day, one that was at Table (to prevent impertinent discourse) said, That it was a question whether they should all go to Heaven or no, which struck them all into a dump, and caused every one to enter into a serious consideration with themselves, one thought

Prov. 15. 23. 25. c. 11. A word spoken (*gnalophnan*) upon his wheels, that is with a due concurrence and observation of all circumstances of time, place, person, all which are as the wheels upon which our words & speeches should run, such a word is like apples of gold in pictures of silver.

A 3   if

The Epistle

if any of this company go to Hell, it must bee I, and so thought another, and another, and indeed so thought almost every one then present, as well servants that waited, as those that sate at Table, as it was afterwards acknowledged, and (through the mercy and blessing of God) this speech so wrought upon the spirits of most of them, that it proved the first instrumental means of their conversion.

I have my hopes, through grace, that this Treatise, though it bee sown in weakness, yet by the blessing of the most High upon it, it may rise in power, and bee an instrumental means of the winning of souls to Christ, which is my highest ambition in this world, and therefore I have broke thorow all difficulties, and carnal reasonings, that might otherwise have stifled this babe in the womb, and kept it from ever seeing of the light.

I have read of an Emperour, that delighted in no undertakings, so much as those which in the esteem

of

Dedicatory.

of his Counsellors, and Captains, were deemed most difficult and impossible, if they said such or such an enterprize would never bee accomplished, it was argument enough to him, to make the adventure, and hee usually prospered, hee seldome miscarried.

I have never found greater and choiser blessings to attend any of my poor weak Labours, than those that have been brought forth into the world through the greatest straights and difficulties.

Valerius Maximus reports, that one telling a Souldier, going to war against the Persians, that they would hide the Sun with their Arrows, hee answered, wee shall fight best in the shade; nothing should discourage nor dishearten a souldier of Christ, 2 Tim. 2. 3, 4. Christ saith to all his Souldiers (as the black Prince his Father said to him, fighting as it were in blood to the knees, and in great distress) either vanquish or dye. Men of no resolution, or of weak resolution, will bee but little serviceable to the good

Valerius Maximus. lib. 3. c. de Fiducia.

Hist. of France. p. 196.

The Epistle

good of souls; such watch-men as will bee free from the blood of souls, and bee serviceable to the interest of Christ in turning sinners from darkness to light, must bee men of spirit and resolution.

August. de tempore Serm. 256.

I remember Austin beginneth one of his Sermons thus (Ad vos mihi Sermo, O Juvenes flos etatis, periculum mentis) *To you is my speech, O young men, the flower of age, the danger of the mind.*

So say I, to you, O young men, do I dedicate the ensuing Treatise, and that first, because the matter contained therein, doth primarily and eminently concern you.

And secondly, Because of an earnest desire that I have of your internal and eternal welfare.

And thirdly, Because of some late impulses that have been upon my spirit, to leave this Treatise in your hands as a Legacy of my Love, and as a testimony and witness of my (great) Ambition, to help forward your everlasting salvation.

And

Dedicatory.

And fourthly, Because there is most hope of doing good amongst you (as I evidence more at large in the following Treatise.)

And fifthly, To countermine the great underminer of your souls, whose great design is to poison you, and to possesse you in the morning of your daies.

Sixthly, To provoke others that are more able and worthy to bee more serviceable to you in declaring themselves, fully on this very subject, which none yet have done that I know of, though it bee a point of as great concernment to young persons (especially) as any I know in all the Scriptures.

Seventhly and lastly, Because there are very many that do lye in wait to deceive, corrupt, and poison your persons with God-dishonouring, Christ-denying, conscience-wasting, and soul-damning opinions, principles, and blasphemies.

I have read of one who boasted and gloried in this, that hee had spent thirty years in corrupting and poy-

Eph. 4.14 A blind eye is worse than a lame foot, hee that had the leprosie in his head, was to bee pronounced utterly unclean.

The Epistle

poysoning of youth; doubtless many wretches, many monsters there bee among us, who make it their business, their glory, their all, to delude and draw young persons to those dangerous errours and blasphemies that leads to destruction. Errour and folly (saith one very well) bee the knots of Satan, wherewith hee ties children to the stake to bee burnt in Hell.

There is a Truth in what the Tragædian said long since (Venenum in auro bibitur) Poison is commonly drunk out of a cup of gold; So is an errour or by-notion soonest taken into the judgement and conscience from persons of the fairest carriage, and smoothest conversations. Errour is so foul an Hagge, that if it should come in its own shape, a man would loathe it, and flye from it, as from Hell.

If Jezabel had not painted her face, shee had not gotten so many young doting Adulterers, to have followed her to their own ruine.

Ah! Young men, young men, the

Dedicatory.

the blessing of the Lord upon your serious and diligent perusal of this Treatise, may bee a happy means to preserve you from being ensnared and deluded by those monsters, who compass Sea and Land to make Proselytes for Hell.

Mat. 23. 15.

And thus I have given you the reasons of my dedicating this Treatise to the service of your souls. I would willingly presume that it will bee as kindly taken, as it is cordially tendred; I hope none of you into whose hands it may fall, will say as once Antipater King of Macedonia did, when one presented him with a book treating of Happiness, his answer was (Ou Scholazo) I have no leasure.

Ah! Young men and women, young men and virgins, as you tender the everlasting welfare of your souls, as you would escape Hell, and come to Heaven, as you would have an interest in Christ, a pardon in your bosomes, as you would bee blessed here, and glorious hereafter, finde time, finde leasure, to read over and over the following Treatise

The Epistle

Treatise, which is purposely calculated for your eternal good. But before I go further, I think it needful in some respects, to give the world some further account of other reasons or motives that hath prevailed with mee to appear once more in Print; and they are these.

First, Having preached a Sermon occasionally upon these words (on which this following Discourse is built) I was earnestly importun'd to print the Sermon, by some worthy friends; I did as long as in modesty I could withstand their desires (judging it not worthy of them) but being at last overcome, and setting about the work, the breathings and comings in of God were such, as hath occasioned that one Sermon to multiply into many. Luther tells us, that when hee first began to turn his back upon Popery, hee intended no more, but to withstand Popish Pardons, and selling Indulgencies; yet neither would God, or his enemies let him alone, till hee resolved with Moses not to

leave

Dedicatory.

leave a hoof of Popery unopposed, &c. God many times in the things of the Gospel, carries forth his Servants beyond their intentions, beyond their resolutions. But

Secondly, The kinde acceptance, and good quarter that my other peeces have found in the world, and those signal and multiplied blessings that have followed them, to the winning of many over to Christ, and to the building up of others in Christ, hath encouraged mee to present this Treatise to the World, hoping that the Lord hath a blessing in store for this also. Gracious experiences are beyond notions, and impressions; they are very quickning and encourageing.

Thirdly, That I might in some measure make up others neglects, whose age, whose parts, whose experiences, whose graces, hath long called upon them to do something considerable in this way, and that they may bee provoked by my weak assay to do better, and to make up what is wanting, through

my

The Epistle

my invincible infirmities, and spiritual wants and weaknesses, which are so many, as may well make a sufficient Apology for all the defects and weaknesses that in this Treatise shall appear to a serious judicious eye. But

Fourthly, The love of Christ and souls hath constrained mee to it; as there is an attractive, so there is a compulsive virtue in divine Love. Love to Christ and souls, will make a man willing to spend, and bee spent; hee that praies himself to death, that preaches himself to death, that studies himself to death, that sweats himself to death, for the honour of Christ, and good of souls, shall bee no looser in the end: Divine Love is like a rod of Myrtle, which as Pliny reports, makes the Traveller that carries it in his hand, that hee shall never bee faint or weary. Divine Love is very operative (si non operatur, non est) if it do not work, it is an argument, it is not at all; Divine Love like fire is not idle; but active, hee that

margin:
2 Cor. 5. 14
2 Cor. 12. 15.
Solus amor nescit difficultates.
Love knows no difficulties

Dedicatory.

that loves cannot bee barren; love will make the soul constant and abundant in well-doing. God admits none to Heaven (saith Justin Martyr) but such as can perswade him by their works, that they love him. The very Heathen hath observed, that God doth not love his children, with a weak womanish affection, but with a strong masculine love; and certainly, they that love the Lord strongly, that love him with a Masculine love, they cannot but lay out their little all for him, and his glory. But

Fifthly, I observe that Satan and his instruments are exceeding busie and unwearied in their designs, attempts, and endeavours, in these daies, to corrupt and poison, to defile and destroy the young, the tender, the most hopeful, and most flourishing plants among uss.

Latimer told the Clergy in his time, that if they would not learn diligence, and vigilance, of the Prophets and Apostles, they should learn it of the Devil, who goes up and down

Seneca.

It is said of *Marcellus* the *Roman* General, that hee could not bee quiet (*Nec victor, nec victus*) neither Conquered, nor Conquerer; such a one is Satan.

The Epistle

down his Dioceses, and acts by an untired power, seeking whom hee may destroy; when the Wolves are abroad, the Shepheard should not sleep, but watch; yea double his watch, remembring that hee were better have all the blood of all the men in the world upon him, than the blood of one soul upon him, by his negligence, or otherwise.

Satan is a Lion, not a Lamb, a roaring Lion, not a sleepy Lion, not a Lion standing still, but a Lion going up and down as not being contented with the Prey, the many millions of souls hee hath got, hee seeks whom hee may sip up at a draught, as that word (καταπιη) in the 1 Pet. 5. 8. imports, his greatest design, is to fill Hell with souls, which should awaken every one to bee active, and to do all that may bee done to prevent his design, and to help forward the salvation of souls.

Chrys. in Mat. Ho. 15.

Chrysostome compares good Pastors, to fountains that ever send forth waters, or Conduits that are alwaies running, though no pail bee put under. But Sixthly,

Dedicatory.

Sixthly and lastly, I know the whole life of man is but an hour to work in, and the more work any man doth for Christ on Earth, the better pay hee shall have when hee comes to Heaven. Every man shall at last reap as hee sows; Opportunities of doing service for Christ, and souls, are more worth than a world; therefore I was willing to take hold on this, not knowing how soon I may put off this earthly Tabernacle; and remembring, that as there is no beleeving, nor repenting in the grave, so there is no praying, preaching, writing, nor printing in the grave; wee had need to bee up and doing, to put both hands to it, and to do all wee do with all our might, knowing, that the night draws on upon us, wherein no man can work.

A Christians dying day is the Lords pay day; that is a time to receive wages, not to do work. And thus I have given the World a true account of the Reasons that moved mee to print the following discourse; before I close up, I desire to speak a

1 Cor. 15. ult.

2 Cor. 9.6

2 Pet. 1. 13, 14
Eccl. 9.10

John 9.4

a   word

The Epistle

word to young persons, and another to aged persons, and then I shall take leave of both.

My request to you, who are in the Prim-rose of your daies. is this, if ever the Lord shall be pleased so to owne and Crown, so to bless, and follow this following discourse, as to make it an effectual means of turning you to the Lord, of winning you to Christ, of changing your natures, and converting your souls (for such a thing as that, I pray, hope, and beleeve) that then you would do two things for mee.

First. That you would never cease bearing of mee upon your hearts when you are in the Mount, that I may bee very much under the pourings out of the Spirit, that I may be clear, high, and full in my communion with God, and that I may bee alwaies close, holy, humble harmless, and blameless in my walkings with God; And that his work may more and more prosper in my hand.

Psa. 66. 16
1 Pet. 3. 15.

Secondly That you would by word of mouth, letter, or some other way, acquaint

Dedicatory.

acquaint mee with what the Lord hath done for your souls, if he shall make me a spiritual Father to you; do not hide his grace from me, but acquaint me how he hath made the seed that was sown in weakness, to rise in power upon you, and that

First, That I may do what I can, to help on that work begun upon you, that your penny may become a pound, your mite a million, your drop an ocean.

Secondly, That I may the better English some impressions that have been upon my own spirit, since I begun this work.

Thirdly, That my joy and thankfulness may be increased, and my soul more abundantly engaged to that God, who hath blest the day of small things to you, ponder these scriptures, (2 Cor. 7. 3, 4, 13. Phil. 2. 2. ch. 4. 1. Philemon ver. 7. 2 John 3, 4.) And then be ashamed to declare what the Lord hath done for you, if you can.

Fourthly, It is better to convert one, than to civilize a thousand; and

1 Thes. 2. 19, 20
2 Cor. 9. 2.

Mat. 25. 23.
Dan. 12. 3
Pro. 11. 30

a 2   will

The Epistle

will turn more at last to a Ministers account in that day, wherein hee shall say, Lo here am I, and the children that thou hast given mee, Isa. 8. 18. such a man (with his spiritual children about him) shall look on God with more comfort and boldness, than those that are onely able to say, Lo here am I, and the many Benefices; here am I, and the many Ecclesiastical dignities and glories; here am I, and the many hundreds a year that man had given, and I have gotten. But,

Fifthly and lastly, The conversion of others is a secondary and more remote evidence of a mans own renovation and conversion. Paul was converted himself, before God made him instrumental for others Conversion. Gods usual method is, to convert by them, who are converted.

Act. 9. 3
Isa. 6. 5.
Mal. 2. 5,
6, 7, &c.

I do not remember any one instance in all the Scripture of Gods converting any by such who have not been converted first themselves; yet I know his grace is free, and the wind blows

Dedicatory.

blows where it lists, when it lists, and as it lists.

To aged persons I have a word, and then I have done.

First, To Gray-headed Saints, Ah Friends, ah Fathers, would you see your honour, your happiness, your blessedness! then look into this Treatise, and there you will finde what an unspeakable honour it is to bee an Old Disciple, what a glory it is to bee good betimes, and to continue so to old age.

Secondly, To white-headed Sinners, whose spring is past, whose summer is overpast, and who are arrived at the fall of the leaf, and yet have a Hell to escape, a Christ to beleeve in, sins to pardon, hearts to change, souls to save, and Heaven to make sure; would such bee encouraged from Scripture grounds to repent, beleeve, and hope, that yet there is mercy for such; let them seriously peruse this Treatise, especially the latter part of it, and there they may finde enough to keep them from despairing, and to incourage them to adven-

The Epistle, &c.

adventure their souls upon him that is mighty to save.

There are many things in this Treatise that are of use to all, and several things of moment, that are not every day preached nor read; I have made it as pleasurable as time would permit, that so it might bee the more profitable to the Reader, and that I might the better take the young man by (a holy) craft, which is a high point of heavenly wisdome, there being no wisdome to that of winning of souls. I shall now follow this poor peece with my weak prayers, that it may bee so blest from Heaven, as that it may bring in some, and build up others, and do good to all; And so rest

2 Cor. 12.
ch. 15. 2.
Pro. 11. 30

Your Friend and Servant in the Gospel of Christ,

THOMAS BROOKS.

THE

The Contents.

The explication of the words, from pag. 1. to pag. 10.

Chap. I.

Doct. That is a very desirable and commendable thing for young men to be (really) good betimes, this truth proved. p. 10, 11, 12.
Twelve Reasons of this point,

1 *Because hee commands it, whose commands are not to bee disputed, but obeyed.* from p. 12. to 16

2 *Because they have means and opportunities of being good betimes.* from p. 16. to 20.

3 *Because then they will have fewer sins to answer for, and repent of.* p. 20, 21

4 *Because time is a precious talent that Young men must bee accountable for.* from p. 21. to 26

5 Because

The Contents.

5 Because then they will have the greater comfort and joy when they come to be old. from 26. to 28.

6 Because an eternity of felicity and glory hangs upon those few moments that are allotted to them. from 28. to 33

7 Because they do not begin to live, till they begin to be really good. from 33. to 36

8 Because the promise of finding God, of enjoying God, is made over to an early seeking of God, &c. from 36. to 44

9 Because the time of youth is the choicest and fittest time for service. from 44. to 47

10 Because death may suddenly and unexpectedly seize on youth, youth being as fickle as old age. from 47. to 52

11 Because it is ten to one, nay a hundred to ten, if ever they are converted, if they are not converted when they are young. from 52. to 55

12 Because else they will never attain to the honour of being an Old Disciple. 55, 56

Chap.

The Contents.

Chap. II.

The honour of an Old Disciple, shewed in seven particulars.
1 *All men will honour an old Disciple.* from 56. to 58
2 *God usually reveals himself most to old Disciples, to old Saints,* 58. to 62
3 *An old Christian, an old Disciple, hath got the art of serving God,* 62, 63
4 *An old Disciple, an old Christian, is rich in spiritual experiences.* from 63. to 67
5 *An old Disciple is firm and fixt in his resolutions.* from 67. to 70
6 *An old Disciple is prepared for death.* from 70. to 73
7 *An old Disciple shall have a great reward in Heaven.* from 73. to 79
Use of Reproof. from 79. to 84

Chap. III.

The several evils that most properly attend youth, as
1 *Pride.* from 84. to 87
2 *Sensual pleasures and delights.* from 87. to 93
3 *Rash-*

The Contents.

3 *Rashness.*   *from* 93. *to* 96
4 *Mocking and scoffing at Religious men, and religious things. from* 96. *to* 98
5 *Wantonness.*   *from* 98. *to* 101

Chap. IV.

Use of Exhortation, to exhort young persons to be good betimes, and motives moving thereunto, as

1 *It is a high honour, to be good betimes. from* 102. *to* 106
2 *Christ gave himself for sinners when hee was in the prim-rose of his age. from* 106. *to* 111
3 *It is the best way in the world to bee rich in spiritual experiences. from* 111. *to* 116
4 *The present time is the only time that you are sure of. from* 116. *to* 122
5 *It is just with God to reserve the dregs of his wrath for them, who reserve the dregs of their daies for him. from* 122. *to* 125
6 *The sooner you are good on earth, the greater will be your reward in Heaven. from* 125. *to* 134

7 *The*

The Contents.

7 *The Lord is very much affected and taken with your seeking of him, and following after him in the spring and morning of your youth.* from p. 134. to 136

8 *It will prevent many sad and black temptations.* from p. 136. to 140

9 *Consider the worth and excellency of souls.* from 140. to 144

10 *God will at last bring young men to a reckoning.* from 144. to 155

Chap. V.

Quest. Whether in the great day of account, the sins of the Saints shall bee brought into the judgement of discussion and discovery, or no? the negative proved by divers Arguments. from 155. to 171

Chap. VI.

Directions to such as would be good betimes, as would know and love, seek and serve the Lord in the prim-rose of their daies; as

1 *Take heed of putting the day of death a far*

The Contents.

far off.   *from* 171. *to* 177

2 *If you would bee good betimes, take heed of leaning to your own understanding.*   *from* 177. *to* 182

3 *If you would be good betimes, take heed of flatterers and flattery.*   *from* 182. *to* 191

4 *If you would seek the Lord in the spring and morning of your daies, then take heed of engaged affections to the things of the world. from* 191. *to* 197

5 *If you would be good betimes, then you must take heed betimes of carnal reason, &c.*   *from* 197. *to* 201

6 *Take heed of comparing your selves with those that are worse than your selves.*   *from* 201. *to* 207

Chap. VII.

Secondly, As those six things must be declined, so several other things must be practised; if you would be good betimes, as

1 *If you would be good betimes, then you must labour to be acquainted with four things betimes, as*

1 *You must labour to acquaint your selves with*

The Contents.

with the scripture betimes. 207. to 219

2 *You must acquaint your selves with your selves betimes. from* 219 to 226

3 *If you would be good betimes, then you must acquaint your selves with Jesus Christ betimes. from* 226. to 228

Now there are six things which you should be thorowly acquainted with concerning Jesus Christ. As

1 *If you would be good betimes, then you must know that there is every thing in Christ, that may ecourage you to seek him, and serve him. from* 228. to 230

2 *If you would be good betimes, then you must know betimes, that Jesus Christ is mighty to save. from* 230. to 234

3 *Then you must know betimes, that there is a marvellous readiness and willingness in Christ to imbrace & entertain returning sinners, &c.* 234. to 236

4 *If you would be good betimes, then you must know betimes that Jesus Christ is designed, sealed and appointed by the Father to the office of a Mediatour. from* 236. to 240

5 *If you would be good betimes, then you must know betimes, that there is no way to*

The Contents.

to salvation but by Jesus Christ. 240.
to 246

6 If you would bee good betimes, then you must know betimes, that the heart of Jesus Christ is as much set upon sinners now hee is in Heaven, as ever it was when hee was on Earth. 246. to 249

4 If you would bee good betimes, then
1 You must acquaint your selves with those that are good betimes. 249. to 254

2 If you would be good betimes, then you must shun the occasion of sin betimes. from 254. to 262

3 If you would be good betimes, then you must remember the eye of God betimes. from 262. to 265

4 If you would be good betimes, then you must hearken to the voice of conscience betimes. from 265. to 269

5 If you would be good betimes, then you must know wherein true happiness lies, betimes. from 269. to 272

6 Lastly, If you would be good betimes, then you must break your covenant with sin betimes: Now to work you to that, you must alwaies look upon sin under these six notions. 1 You

The Contents.

1 *You must look upon sin under the notion of an enemy.* from 272. to 277
2 *Under the notion of bonds, &c.* from 277. to 279
3 *Under the notion of fire; six resemblances between sin and fire.* from 279. to 289
4 *Under the notion of a Theef, &c.* from 289. to 292
5 *Under the notion of a burden, &c.* from 292. to 296
6 *Under the notion of a Tyrant, &c.* from 296. to 299

Chap. VIII.

1 Object. *It may be time enough hereafter to seek and serve the Lord, &c.*
This Objection answered four waies.
from 299. to 304
2 Object. *If I should seek and serve the Lord in the spring and morning of my daies, I should lose the love and favour of such and such friends and relations,*
Four Answers to this Objection, &c.
from 304. to 311
3 Object. *I shall meet with many reproaches.* Eight

The Contents.

Eight Answers to this Objection. from 311. to 326

4 *Object. Most men give liberty to themselves, and walk in waies more pleasing to the flesh.*

This Objection answered five waies. from 326. to 339

5 *Object. The last (I shall mention) is, that God is a God of mercy, in him are bowels of mercy, yea, a Sea, an Ocean of mercy, hee delights in mercy, &c.*

Five Answers to this Objection. from 339. to 349.

Chap. IX.

Lastly, The Old mans doubts resolved, in eight several answers. from 349. to the end.

THE

THE
Young-Mans Duty
AND
EXCELLENCY.

1 KING. 14. ch. 13. v.

And all Israel shall mourn for him, and bury him: for hee only of Jeroboam shall come to the grave, because in him there is found some good thing toward the Lord God of Israel, in the house of Jeroboam.

I SHALL onely stand upon the latter part of this Verse, because that affords me matter most suitable to my design.

--Be-

The Young Mans Duty

-- Because in him there is found some good thing toward the Lord God of Israel, *in the house of* Jeroboam.

These words are a commendation of *Abijahs* life, *in him was found some good thing toward the Lord*, &c. when *Abijah* was a Childe, *verf.* 3. 12. when hee was in his young and tender years, hee had the feeds of grace in him, hee had the Image of God upon him, hee could difcern between good and evil, and hee did that which pleafed the Lord.

The Hebrew word (Nagnar) tranflated Childe, *verf.* 3. is very often applied to fuch as wee call Youth, or young men, *Exod.* 24. 5. *Numb.* 6. 11. 1 *Sam.* 2. 17, &c.

Of fuch age and prudence, was *Abijah*, as that hee could chufe good, and refufe evil, hee was a *Lot* in *Sodome*, hee was good among the bad, the bent and frame of his heart was towards that which was good, when the heart both of his Father and Mother was

נַעַר

Is ufed for a young man, or ftripling, Gen. 22. 5. and often for a fervant, though he bee a man of ripe years, Eft. 2. 2. Such as one Evangelift calleth young men, Luk. 12. 45. another calleth fellow-fervants, Mat. 24. 49.

and Excellency. 3

was set upon evil. *Abijah* began to bee good betimes, hee crost that pestilent Proverb, *a young Saint, and an old Devil.* 'Tis the glory and goodnesse of God, that hee will take notice of the least good that is in any of his, 1 *Pet.* 3. 6. There was but one good word in *Sarah's* speech to *Abraham,* and that was this, shee called him *Lord,* and this God mentions for her honour and commendation, *shee called him Lord*: God looks more upon one grain of Wheat, than upon a heap of Chaff; upon one shining Pearl, than upon a heap of rubbish. God findes a Pearl in *Abijah,* and hee puts it into his Crown, to his eternal Commendation. *There was found in him some good thing toward the Lord,* &c. For the words,

There was found in him, The Hebrew word *Matsa,* sometimes signifies finding without seeking, *Isa.* 65. 1. *I am found of them that sought mee not,* so *Psal.* 116. *vers.* 3. *The sorrows of death compassed mee,*

B 2 *and*

and the pains of hell got hold upon me, I found trouble and sorrow. I found trouble which I look'd not for, I was not searching after sorrow, but I found it. There's an elegancy in the Original. The pains of Hell gat hold upon mee; So wee read, but the Hebrew is, The pains of Hell found mee (one word signifies both) they found mee, I did not find them. *There was found in Abijah some good thing towards the Lord, i.e.* there was found in him without searching, or seeking, some good thing towards the Lord, it was plain and visible enough, men might see and observe it without enquiring, or seeking, they might runne and read some good thing in him towards the Lord.

Secondly, The word sometime signifies, finding by seeking or inquiry, *Isa.* 55. 6. *Seek yee the Lord while hee may bee found, &c.* So upon search and inquiry, there was found in *Abijah* (though young) some good thing toward the Lord.

Thirdly,

and Excellency.

Thirdly, Sometimes the word notes the obtaining of that which is sufficient, *Josh.* 17. 16. *Numb.* 11. 22. *Judg.* 21. 14. in *Abijah* there was that good in him towards the Lord, that was sufficient to evidence the work of grace upon him, sufficient to satisfie himself and others, of the goodness, and happiness of his condition; though hee died in the prime, and flower of his daies, &c.

And in him was found some good thing; the Hebrew word (*Tob*) that is here rendred good, signifies,

First, That which is right and just, *2 Sam.* 15. 3. See thy matters are good and right, *i. e.* just and right.

Secondly, That which is profitable, *Deut.* 6. 11. *Houses full of all good things i. e.* houses full of all profitable things.

Thirdly, That which is pleasing, *2 Sam.* 19. 27. *Do what is good in thine eyes, i. e.* do what is pleasing in thine eyes.

B 3   Fourth-

Fourthly, That which is full and compleat, *Gen. 15. 15. Thou shalt bee buried in a good old age*, i. e. thou shalt be buried when thine age is full and compleat.

Fifthly, That which is joyful and delightful, 1 *Sam. 25. 8. wee come in a good day*, i. e. wee come in a joyful and delightful day; now put all together, and you may see that there was found in *Abijah* when hee was young, that which was right and just, that which was pleasing and profitable, and that which was matter of joy and delight.

In the Words you have two things that are most considerable.

First, That this young mans goodness was towards the Lord God of *Israel*; many there are that are good, nay, very good towards men, who yet are bad, yea, very bad towards God. Some there are who are very kinde to the creature, and yet very unkinde to their Creator; many mens goodness

This age affords many such Hypocrites, such Monsters, &c.

and Excellency.

nefs towards the creature is like the rifing Sun, but their goodnefs towards the Lord is like a morning Cloud, or as the early dew, which is foon dried up by the Sun-beams, but *Abijah's* goodneffe was towards the Lord, his goodneffe faced the Lord, it look't towards the glory of God. Two things makes a good Chriftian, good actions, and good aims; And though a good aim doth not make a bad action good, (as in *Uzzah*) yet a bad aim makes a good action bad (as in *Jehu*) whofe juftice was approved, but his policy punifhed, the firft Chapter of *Hofea*, and the fourth verfe, doubtleffe *Abijahs* actions were good, and his aims good; and this was indeed his glory, that his goodneffe was towards the Lord.

It's recorded of the *Calanenfes*, that they made a ftately monument of Kingly magnificence, in remembrance of two Sons, who took their aged Parents upon

Hof. 6. 4.

There may be *Malum opus in bona materia*, as in *Jehues* zeal.

their

The Young Mans Duty

their backs, and carried them through the fire, when their Fathers house was all in a flame; these young men were good towards their Parents; but what is this to *Abijahs goodness towards the Lord*, &c? A man cannot bee good towards the Lord, but hee will bee good towards others; but a man may bee good towards others, that is not good towards the Lord: Oh that mens practises did not give too loud a Testimony every day to this assertion! &c.

Secondly, Hee was good among the bad, *Hee was good in the house of Jeroboam*; 'tis in fashion to seem (at least) to bee good among the good; but to bee really good among those that are bad, that are eminently bad, argues not only a truth of goodness, but a great degree of goodness; this young man was good, *in the house of Jeroboam, who made all Israel to sin*; who was naught, who was very naught, who was stark naught: and yet

Happy are those souls that with the Sturgion or Crab-fish can swim against the stream of custome and example, and that with Atticus, can cleave to the right, though losing side.

and Excellency.   9

yet *Abijah*, as the Fishes which live in the Salt-Sea are fresh; so though he lived in a (sink) a sea of wickedness, yet hee retained his *goodness towards the Lord.*

They say Roses grow the sweeter, when they are planted by Garlick: they are sweet and rare Christians indeed, who hold their goodness, and grow in goodness where wickedness sits on the throne; and such a one the young man in the Text was.

To bee Wheat among Tares, Corn among Chaffe, Pearls among Cockles, and Roses among Thorns, is excellent.

To bee a *Jonathan* in *Sauls* Court, to bee an *Obadiah* in *Ahabs* Court, to bee an *Abedmelech* in *Zedechias* Court, and to be an *Abijah* in *Jeroboams* Court, is a wonder, a miracle.

To bee a *Lot* in *Sodome*, to bee an *Abraham* in *Chaldæa*, to bee a *Daniel* in *Babylon*, to bee a *Nehemiah* in *Damasco*, and to bee a *Job* in the Land of *Husse*, is to bee a Saint among

mong Devils, and such a one the young man in the Text was.

The Poëts affirm, that *Venus* never appeared so beautious as when shee sate by black *Vulcans* side. Gracious souls shine most clear when they be set by black-conditioned persons. *Stephens* face never shin'd so Angelically, so gloriously (in the Church) where all were virtuous, as before the Council, where all were vicious and malicious. So *Abijah* was a bright Star, a shining Sun in *Jeroboams* Court, which for prophaneness and wickedness, was a very hell.

The words that I have chosen to insist upon, will afford us several observations, but I shall onely name one, which I intend to prosecute at this time, and that is this, *viz.*

CHAP. I.

Doct. *That it is a very desirable and commendable thing for young men to be really good betimes.*

Other

and Excellency. XI

OTher Scriptures speak out this to bee a truth, besides what you have in the Text to confirm it, as that of the second of *Chronicles*, Chap. 34. 1, 2, 3. verses. *Josiah* was eight years old when hee began to reign, and hee reigned in *Jerusalem* one and thirty years. And hee did that which was right in the sight of the Lord, and walked in the waies of *David* his Father, and declined neither to the right hand, nor to the left; for in the eighth year of his reign, while hee was yet young, hee began to seek after the God of *David* his Father: and in the twelfth year, hee began to purge *Judah*, and *Jerusalem*, from the high places, and the Groves, and the carved Images, and the Molten Images. 'Twas *Obadiah*'s honour, that hee feared the Lord from his youth. And *Timothies* Crown, that hee knew the Scripture from a Childe; and *Johns* Joy, that hee found Children walking in the truth;

Job 32. 4, 5, 6, 7.

1 King. 18. 12.
2 Tim. 3. 15.
2 Epist. 4. v.

truth; this revived his good old heart, and made it dance for joy in his bosome; to spend further time in the proving of this truth, would be but to light Candles, to see the Sun at Noon.

The grounds and Reasons of this point, *viz.*

That it is a very desirable and commendable thing for young men to bee really good betimes; are these that follow.

Reason I.

First, Because the Lord commands it; and divine Commands are not to be disputed, but obeyed. In the 12 Chapter of *Ecclesiastes*, and the 1 verse, *Remember now thy Creator in the daies of thy youth, while the evil daies come not, nor the years draw nigh, when thou shalt say, I have no pleasure in them:* Remember now; I say now: now is an atome, it will puzzle the wisdome of a Philosopher, the skill of an Angel to divide: Now, is a Monosyllable in all Learned Languages.

Marginal notes: Deut. 6.5. ch. 11. 13. *Augustine beginneth one of his Sermons thus (Ad vos mihi Sermo, O juvenes, flos ætatis, periculum mentis. August. de tempore Serm. 246.* To you is my speech O young men, the flower of age, the danger of the mind.)

Remember now thy Creator: Remember him presently, instantly, for thou dost not know what a day, what an hour may bring forth; thou canst not tell what deadly sin, what deadly temptation, what deadly judgement may over-take thee; if thou dost not now, even now *remember thy Creator.*

Remember now thy Creator: Remember to know him, remember to love him, remember to desire him, remember to delight in him, remember to depend upon him, remember to get an interest in him, remember to live to him, and remember to walk with him. *Remember now thy Creator*, the Hebrew is *Creatours*, Father, Son, and Spirit. To the making of man, a Council was called in Heaven, in the first of *Genesis*, and 29 vers. *Remember thy Creatours*, remember the father, so as to know him, so as to bee inwardly acquainted with him. Remember the Son, so as to beleeve in him, so as to rest upon him,

him so as to embrace him, and so as to make a compleat resignation of thy self to him. Remember the Spirit, so as to hear his voice, so as to obey his voice, so as to feel his presence, and so as to experience his influence, &c.

Remember now thy Creator in the daies of thy youth; hee doth not say, in the time of thy youth, but *in the daies of thy youth*, to note, that our life is but as a few daies; 'tis but a vapour, a span, a flower, a shadow, a dream; and therefore *Seneca* saith well, *that though death bee before the Old mans face, yet hee may bee as near the Young mans back*, &c.

Aug. l. 1. Confess.

Mans life is the shadow of smoak, the dream of a shadow; one doubteth whether to call it a dying life, or a living death.

Ah! Young men, God commands you to bee good betimes. Remember, young men, that it is a dangerous thing to neglect one of his Commands, who by another is able to command

and Excellency.

mand you into nothing, or into Hell. To act or run cross to Gods express Command (though under pretence of Revelation from God) is as much as a mans life is worth, as you may see in that sad story, 1 *King.* 13. 24. *vers.* &c.

Let Young men put all their carnal Reasons, though never so many and weighty, into one scale, and Gods absolute Command in the other, and then write *Tekel* upon all their reasons; they are weighed in the ballance, and found too light.

Ah Sirs! what God commands must bee put in speedy execution, without denying, or delaying, or disputing the difficulties that attend it. Most young men in these daies do as the Heathens, when their gods called for a man, they offered a Candle; or as *Hercules* offered up a painted man instead of a living. When God calls upon young men to serve him with the Primrose of their youth, they usually put him off till

Obedientia non discutit Dei mandata, sed facit. Prosper.

till they are overtaken with trembling joynts, dazled eies, fainting hearts, failing hands, and feeble knees, but this will be bitterness in the end, &c.

Reason II.
Because they have means and opportunities of being good betimes.

<small>Young men must bee really good betimes.</small>

Never had men better means, and greater opportunities of being good, of doing good, and of receiving good than now. Ah Lord! how knowing, how beleeving, how holy, how heavenly, how humble might young men bee, were they not wanting to their own souls? Young men might bee good, very good, yea eminently good, would they but improve the means of grace, the tenders of mercy, and the knockings of Christ by his Word, Works and Spirit.

<small>*Erasmus.*</small>

The Antients painted Opportunity with a hairy fore-head, but bald behinde, to signifie, that while a man hath opportunity before him,

and Excellency.

him, hee may lay hold on it, but if hee suffer it to slip away, he cannot pull it back again.

How many young men are now in everlasting chains, who would give ten thousand worlds, (had they so many in their hands to give) to enjoy but an opportunity to hear one Sermon more, to make one Prayer more, to keep one Sabbath more, but cannot? this is their Hell, their Torment, this is the Scorpion that is still biting, this is the Worm that is alwaies gnawing. Woe, woe, to us, that wee have neglected and trifled away those golden opportunities that once wee had to get our sins pardoned, our natures changed, our hearts bettered, our consciences purged, and our souls saved, &c. * I have read of a King, who having no issue to succeed him, espying one day a well-favoured youth, took him to Court, and committed him to Tutors, to instruct him, providing by his will, that if hee pro-

* Bellarm. In concione de cruciatibus Gehennæ.

C ved

ed fit for government, hee should bee crowned King, if not, hee should bee bound in chains, and made a Gally-slave. Now when hee grew to years, the Kings executors perceiving that hee had sadly neglected those meanes and opportunities, whereby hee might have been fit for State-Government, called him before them, and declared the Kings will and pleasure concerning him, which was accordingly performed, for they caused him to bee fettered, and committed to the Gallies. Now what tongue can expresse how much hee was affected and afflicted, with his sad and miserable state, especially when hee considered with himself, that now hee is chained, who might have walked at liberty; Now hee is a slave, who might have been a King; now hee is over-ruled by Turks, who might once have ruled over Christians? The Application is easie.

Ah!

and Excellency.

Ah! young men, young men, shall Satan take all opportunities to tempt you? Shall the World take all opportunities to allure you? shall wicked men take all opportunities to ensnare you, and to undo you? and shall Christian friends take all opportunities to better you? and shall Gods faithful Messengers take all opportunities to save you? and will you? *will you neglect so great salvation?* Plutarch writes of *Hannibal*, that when hee could have taken *Rome*, hee would not, and when hee would have taken *Rome*, hee could not. Many in their youthful daies, when they might have Mercy, Christ, Pardon, Heaven, they will not, and in old age, when they would have Christ, Pardon, Peace, Heaven, they cannot, they may not. God seems to say as *Thesius* said once, Go saies hee, and tell *Creon*, *Thesius* offers thee a gracious offer, Yet I am pleased to bee friends, if thou wilt submit (this is my first

C 2   mes-

'Tis storied of Charles King of Sicily and Jerusalem, that hee was called Carolus Cunctator, Charls the lingerer; this age affords many such lingerers, &c.

Why young men should bee really good betimes. Lord, saith Austin, I have loved thee late; the greater was his sin, and the more were his sorrows.

message) but if this offer prevail not, look for mee to bee up in arms.

Reason III.

Because when they have fewer and lesser sins to answer for, and repent of, multitudes of sins and sorrows are prevented by being good betimes.

The more wee number our daies, the fewer sins wee shall have to number. As a copy is then safest from blotting, when dust is put upon it; so are wee from sinning, when (in the time of our youth) wee remember that wee are but dust. The tears of young penitents do more scorch the Devils, than all the flames of Hell, for hereby all their hopes are blasted, and the great underminer countermined, and blown up. *Mane* is the Devils Verb, hee bids tarry, time enough to repent; but *Mane* is Gods Adverb, hee bids repent early, in the morning of thy youth; for then thy sins will bee fewer.

and Excellency.

fewer, and leſſer. Well, young men, remember this, hee that will not at the firſt hand buy good counſel cheap, ſhall at the ſecond hand buy repentance over dear.

Ah! young men, young men, if you do not begin to bee good betimes, thoſe ſinnes that are now as Jewels ſparkling in your eyes, will at laſt bee mil-ſtones about your necks, to ſink you for ever. --Among many things that *Beza* in his laſt Will and Teſtament, gave God thanks for, this was the firſt and chief, that hee at the age of ſixteen years, had called him to the knowledge of the truth, and ſo prevented many ſinnes and ſorrows that otherwiſe would have overtaken him, and have made his life leſſe happy, and more miſerable. Young Saints often prove old Angels, but old ſinners ſeldome prove good Saints, &c.

Pſal. 25.7
Job 13.26

There is nothing puts a more ſerious frame into a mans ſpirit, than to know the worth of his time. Why young men ſhould bee really good betimes.

Reaſon IV.

Becauſe time is a precious Talent that young men muſt bee count-

countable for. The sooner they begin to bee good, the more easie will bee their accounts, especially as to that great Talent of time. *Cato* and other heathens held, that account must bee given, not onely of our labour, but also of our leisure; at the great day it will appear, that they that have spent their time in mourning, have done better than they that have spent their time in dancing; and they that have spent many daies in humiliation, than they that have spent many daies in idle recreations.

I have read of a devout man, who when hee heard a clock strike, hee would say, here is one hour more past that I have to answer for. Ah! young men, as time is very precious, so it is very short, time is very swift, it is suddenly gone, in the 9th. of *Job*, and the 25. vers. *My daies are swifter than a Post, they flee away, they see no good.* The Hebrew word (*Kalal*) translated *swifter than*

and Excellency.

than a Post, signifies any thing that is light, becaufe light things are quick in motion.

The Antients emblem'd time with wings, as it were, not running, but flying. Time is like the Sun, that never ftands ftill, but is ftill a running his race; the Sun did once ftand ftill, yea went back, but fo did never Time. Time is ftill running and flying; it is a bubble, a fhadow, a dream; can you ferioufly confider of this, young men, and not *begin to bee good betimes?* Surely you cannot. Sirs, if the whole earth whereupon wee tread, were turned into a lump of gold, it were not able to purchafe one minute of time. Oh the regreetings of the damned, for mif-fpending precious time! Oh what would they not give to bee free, and to enjoy the means of grace one hour! Ah with what attention! with what intention! with what trembling and melting of heart! with what hungring and thirfting would they hear the word!

Sophocles. Phocilides

Who is there among us that knows how to value time and prize a day at a due rate? *Sen. Epi.*

The Young Mans Duty

Word! Time (saith *Bernard*) were a good commodity in Hell, and the traffick of it most gainful, where, for one day a man would give ten thousand worlds, if he had them; young men, can you in good earnest beleeve this, and not begin to bee good betimes?

Ah! young men and women, as you love your precious immortal souls, as you would escape Hell, and come to Heaven, as you would bee happy in life, and blessed in death, and glorious after death, don't spend any more of your precious time, in drinking and drabbing, in carding, dicing and dancing, don't trifle away your time, don't swear away your time, don't whore away your time, do not lye away your time, but begin to be good betimes, because Time is a Talent, that God will reckon with you for: Ah! young men and women, you may reckon upon years, many years yet to come, when possibly you have not

A Heathen said, hee lived no day without a line, that is, hee did something remarkable every day.

not so many hours to make ready your accompts, it may bee this night you may have a summons, and then if your time bee done, and your work to bee begun, in what a sad case will you bee, will you not wish that you had never been born?

Seneca was wont to jeer the *Jews* for their ill husbandry, in that they lost one day in seven; meaning their Sabbath; O that it were not too true of the most of professors, both young and old, that they lose not onely one day in seven, but several daies in seven.

Sirs! Time let slip cannot bee recalled; the foolish Virgins found it so, and *Saul* found it so, and *Herod* found it so, and *Nero* found it so; the *Israelites* found it so, yea, and *Jacob*, and *Josiah*, and *David*, (though good men) yet they found it so to their cost.

Mat. 25. 5
Judg. 3. 23
Heb. 3. 17, 18, 19.

The *Egyptians* draw the picture of Time with three heads, the first of a greedy Wolf, gapeing, for time past, because it hath rave-

26   *The Young Mans Duty*

ravenously devoured the memory of so many things past recalling. The

Second of a crowned Lion, roaring, for time present, because it hath the principality of all actions, for which it calls loud. The

Third of a Deceitful Dogge, fawning, for time to come, because it feeds some men with many flattering hopes to their eternal undoing: Ah! young men and women, as you would give up your accounts at last with joy, concerning this talent of time, with which God hath trusted you, *begin to bee good betimes*, &c.

Reason 5.

Because they will have the greater comfort and joy when they come to bee old.

The 71. *Psalm* 5. 17, 18. compared. *Thou art my hope, O Lord God, thou art my trust from my youth. O God thou hast taught mee*

Margin note: Why young men should bee really good betimes. *Seneca* (though a Heathen) could say, beleeve mee, true joy is no light thing

mee from my youth, and hitherto I have declared thy wondrous works; Now also when I am old and gray-headed, O God forsake mee not, until I have shewed thy strength unto this Generation, and thy power unto every one that is to come.

   Polycarpus could say, when old, Thus many years have I served my Master Christ, and hitherto hath hee dealt well with mee; if early converts live to bee old, no joy to their joy, their joy will bee the greatest joy, a joy like to the joy of harvest, a joy like to their joy that divide the spoil, their joy will bee the soundest joy, the weightiest joy, the holiest joy, the purest joy, the strongest joy, and the most lasting joy; the carnal joy of the wicked, the glistering (golden) joy of the worldling, and the flashing joy of the hypocrite, is but as the crackling of thorns under a pot, to the joy and comfort of such, who when old, can say with good *Obadiah*, that they feared the Lord from

Isa. 9. 3.

from their youth. If when you are young, your eies shall bee full of tears (for sin) when you are old, your heart shall bee full of joyes. Such shall have the best Wine at last.

Oh! *That young men would begin to bee good betimes,* that so they may have the greater harvest of joy, when they come to bee old, &c. 'tis sad to bee sowing your seed, when you should be reaping your harvest; 'tis best to gather in the Summer of youth, against the Winter of old age.

Why young men should bee really good betimes. Luk. 10. 25.

Reason VI.

Because an eternity of felicity and glory, hangs upon those few moments that are allotted to them.

It was a good question the young man proposed, *What shall I do to inherit eternal life?* I know I shall bee eternally happy, or eternally miserable, eternally blest, or eternally curst, eternally saved, or eternally damned, &c.

and Excellency.

O what shall I do to inherit eternal life! my cares, my fears, my troubles are all about eternity, no time can reach eternity, no age can extend to eternity, no tongue can expresse eternity. Eternity is that (*unum perpetuum hodie*) one perpetual day which shall never have end; what shall I do, what shall I not do, that I may be happy to all eternity?

I am now young, and in the flower of my daies; but who knows what a day may bring forth? the greatest weight hangs upon the smallest wyers, an eternity depends upon those few hours, I am to breath in this World; O what cause have I therefore to bee good betimes, to know God betimes, to beleeve betimes, to repent betimes, to get my peace made, and my pardon sealed betimes, to get my nature changed, my conscience purged, and my interest in Christ cleared betimes, before eternity overtakes mee; before my glasse bee out, my

Æternitas est semper & immutabile esse. The old *Romans* were out, that thought Eternity dwelt in Statues, and in Marble Monuments.

my Sun set, my race run, lest the dark night of eternity should overtake mee, and I made miserable for ever.

I have read of one (*Myrogenes*) who when great gifts were sent unto him, hee sent them all back again, saying, I onely desire this one thing at your Masters hand; to pray for mee, that I may bee saved for eternity. O that all young men and women, who make earth their heaven, pleasures their Paradise, that eat the fat, and drink the sweet, that cloathe themselves richly, and crown their heads with Rose-buds, that they would seriously consider of eternity, so as to hear as for eternity, and pray as for eternity, and live as for eternity, and provide as for eternity! That they may say with that famous Painter *Zeuxes*, (*Æternitati pingo*) I paint for eternity; we do all for eternity, wee beleeve for eternity, we repent for eternity, we obey for eternity, &c.

O that you would not make those

Luke 15. 19, 20.

those things eternal for punishment, that cannot bee eternal for use.

Ah! young men and women, God calls, and the blood of Jesus Christ calls, and the Spirit of Christ in the Gospel calls, and the rage of Satan calls, and your sad state and condition calls, and the happiness and blessedness of glorified Saints calls; these all call aloud upon you to make sure a glorious eternity, before you sail out into that dreadful Ocean. All your eternal good depends upon the short and uncertain moments of your lives; and if the threed of your lives should bee cut, before a happy eternity is made sure, woe to you that ever you were born; Do not say, O young man, that thou art young, and hereafter will bee time enough to provide for eternity, for eternity may bee at the door, ready to carry thee away for ever. Every daies experience speaks out eternity to bee as neer the young mans back, as

Cur ea quæ ad usum diuturna esse non possunt, ad supplicium diuturna deposcet? Ambrose in Luk. 4. T. 5.

as 'tis before the Old mans face.

O graspe to day the diadem of a blessed eternity, left thou art cut off before the morning comes! though there is but one way to come into this world, yet there is a thousand thousand waies to bee sent out of this world; Well young men and women, remember this, as the motions of the soul are quick, so are the motions of divine Justice quick also; and if you will not hear the voice of God to day, if you will not provide for eternity to day, God may swear to morrow that you shall never enter into his rest; it is a very sad and dangerous thing to trifle and dally with God, his word, his offers, our own souls and eternity: Therefore let all young people labour to bee good betimes, and not to let him that is goodness it self alone, till hee hath made them good, till hee hath given them those hopes of eternity that will both make them good, and keep them good,

Heb. 3. 7, 8, 15, 16, 18, 19.

good; that will make them happy, and keep them happy, and that for ever; if all this will not do, then know, that ere long those fears of eternity, of misery, that beget that monster, Despair, which like *Medusa*'s head, astonisheth with its very aspect, and strangles hope, which is the breath of the soul, will certainly overtake you; as it is said, *Dum Spiro, Spero*, so it may bee inverted, *Dum Spero, Spiro*, other miseries may wound the spirit, but despair kills it dead; my prayer shall bee, that none of you may ever experience this sad truth, but that you may all bee good in good earnest betimes, which will yeeld you two Heavens, a Heaven on Earth, and a Heaven after death.

Reason VII.

Because they do not begin to live, till they begin to be really good.

Till they begin to be good, they are

Why young persons should bee really good betimes.

are dead God-wards, and Christ-wards, and Heaven-wards, and Holiness-wards, till a man begins to bee really good, hee is really dead, *Philippians* 2. 1. and that first in respect of working, his works are called dead works, *Hebrews* 9. 14. the most glistering services of unregenerate persons, are but dead works, because they proceed not from a principle of life, and they lead to death, *Rom.* 6. 21. and leave a sentence of death upon the soul, till it bee washed off by the blood of the Lamb.

Respectu operis.

Secondly, Hee is dead in respect of honour, hee is dead to all priviledges, hee is not fit to inherit mercy; who will set the Crown of Life upon a dead man? The Crown of Life is onely for living Christians, *Revelations* 2. 10. The young Prodigal was dead, till hee begun to bee good, till he begun to remember his Fathers house, and to resolve to return home. *My Son was dead, but is alive,*

Respectu honoris.

Luke 15. 24.

alive, and the Widow that liveth in pleasure, is dead while shee liveth.

When *Josaphat* asked *Barlaam*, how old hee was, hee answered, five and forty years old, to whom *Josaphat* replied, thou seemest to bee seventy, true saith hee, if you reckon ever since I was born; but I count not those years which were spent in vanity.

Ah Sirs! you never begin to live, till you begin to bee good in good earnest. There is the life of vegetation, and that is the life of plants; Secondly, there is the life of sense, and that is the life of beasts; Thirdly, there is the life of reason, and that is the life of man; Fourthly, there is the life of grace, and that is the life of Saints; and this life you do not begin to live, till you begin to bee good: If a living Dogge is better than a dead Lion, as the wise man speaks, and if a Fly is more excellent than the Heavens, because the Fly hath

margin:
1 Tim. 5. 6
As it is a reproach to an old man to be in Coats, so tis a disgrace to be an old babe, *i.e.* to be but a babe in grace, when old in years. Heb. 5. 12, 13, 14.

Eccl. 9. 4.

hath life, which the heavens have not, as the Philosopher saith; what a sad dead poor nothing is that person that is a stranger to the life of grace and goodness, that is dead even whilst he is alive?

Most men will bleed, sweat, vomit, purge, part with an estate, yea with a limb, I limbs, yea, and many a better thing, (*viz.* the honour of God, and a good conscience) to preserve their natural lives: as hee cries out, Give mee any deformity, any torment, any misery, so you spare my life; and yet how few, how very few are to bee found, who make it their work, their businesse, to attain to a life of goodnesse, or to begin to bee good betimes, or to bee dead to the world, and alive to God, rather than to bee dead to God, and alive to the world? this is for a lamentation, and shall be for a lamentation that natural life is so highly prized, and spiritual life so little regarded, &c.

Mæcenas in Seneca had rather live in many diseases, than die. And *Homer* reporteth of his *Achilles*, that he had rather bee a servant to a poor Country clown here, than to bee a King to all the souls departed.

Reason

and Excellency.

Reason VIII.

Because the promise of finding God, of enjoying God, is made over to an early seeking of God.

Prov. 8. 17. *I love them that love mee, and they that seek mee early, shall finde me.* Or as the Hebrew hath it, they that seek mee in the morning shall finde mee, by the benefit of the morning light wee come to finde the things wee seek. *Shahhar* signifies to seek inquisitively, to seek diligently, to seek timely in the morning. As the *Israelites* went early in the morning to seek for Manna. And as Students rise early in the morning, and sit close to it, to get knowledge; so saith wisdome, *they that seek mee in the spring and morning of their youth, shall finde mee.*

Now to *seek the Lord early*, is to seek the Lord firstly. God hath in himself all the good of Angels, of men, and universal nature; hee hath all glories, all dignities, all riches, all treasures,

D 3   all

Why young persons should bee really good betimes.

שחר
Exod. 16. 21.
Scipio went first to the Capitol, and then to the Senate. *Tully*, an Heathen, frequently called God, *Optimum maximum*, the best, and greatest. God is *omnis super omnia*.

all pleasures, all comforts, all delights, all joyes, all beatitudes. God is that one infinite perfection in himself, which is eminently and virtually all perfections of the creatures, and therefore hee is firstly to be sought. Abstracts do better expresse him, than Concretes and Adjectives; he is, being, bonity, power, wisdome, justice, mercy, goodness, and love it self, and therefore worthy to be sought before all other things. Seek yee first the good things of the minde, saith *Philosophy*, and doth not Divinity say as much?

Again, To seek early, is to seek opportunely, to seek while the opportunity does present, *Judg.* 9. 33. *Thou shalt rise early, and set upon the City*, that is, thou shall opportunely set upon the City.

Such there have been, who by giving a glass of water opportunely, have obtained a Kingdome, as you may see in the story of *Thamastus*, and King *Agrippa*.

Ah!

Cicero.

Daies of grace have their dates, there take heed of saying, *Cras, Cras,* to morrow to morrow

Ah! Young Men and Women, you do not know, but that by an early, by an opportune seeking of God, you may obtain a Kingdome that shakes not, and glory that passeth not away.

Heb. 12. 28

There is a season wherein God may bee found, *Seek yee the Lord while hee may bee found, call yee upon him while hee is near*, and if you slip this season, you may seek him, and miss him. *Though they cry unto mee, I will not hearken unto them; when yee make many Prayers, I will not hear. Then shall they cry unto the Lord, but hee will not hear. Then shall they call upon mee, but I will not answer, they shall seek mee early, but shall not finde mee.* This was *Sauls* misery; *The Philistims are upon mee, and God will not answer mee*; 'tis justice that they should seek and not finde at last, who might have found, had they but sought seasonably and opportunely, &c.

Isa. 55. 6.

Jer. 11.11
Isa. 1. 15.
Mic. 3. 4.
Prov.1.28

Again,

40 *The Young Mans Duty*

Again, to seek early, is to seek earnestly, affectionately. *With my soul have I desired thee in the night, yea with my spirit within mee will I seek thee early:* The Hebrew word signifies both an earnest, and an early seeking; in the morning, the spirits are up, and men are earnest, lively, and affectionate.

Ah! such a seeking shall certainly bee crowned with finding: *My voice shalt thou hear in the morning, O Lord, in the morning will I direct* (Heb. martial) *my prayer unto thee, and will look up,* (Hebrew, look out like a watchman) *Let all those that put their trust in thee, rejoyce, let them ever shout for joy; because thou defendest them* (Hebrew, thou coverest over, or protectest them) *Let them also that love thy Name, bee joyful in thee: for thou, Lord, wilt bless the righteous, with favour wilt thou compasse him* (Hebrew crown him) *as with a shield.* None have ever thus sought the Lord, but they have, or certainly shall finde

Isa. 26. 9.

Psal. 5. 3. 11. 12.

אֶעֱרָךְ
וַאֲצַפֶּה

and Excellency. 41

finde him. *Seek and yee shall finde,* Matth. 7. 7. *your hearts shall live that seek God,* Psal. 69. 32. *The effectual fervent prayer of a righteous man availeth much,* James 5. 16. or as the Greek hath it; *The working prayer of a righteous man availeth much;* that prayer that sets the whole man a work, will work wonders in Heaven, in the heart, and in the earth. Earnest prayer, like *Sauls* sword, and *Jonathans* bow, never returns empty.

ἐνεργȣμένη. It signifies such a working as notes the liveliest activity that can be.

One speaking of *Luther*, who was a man very earnest in prayer, said (*hic homo potuit apud Deum quod voluit*) this man could have what hee would of God, &c.

Again, to seek early, is to seek chiefly, primarily, after this or that thing; what wee first seek, wee seek as chief. Now to seek the Lord early, is to seek him primarily, chiefly, in the 63 *Psalm,* and the 1 *verse, Thou art my God, early will I seek thee,* that is, I will seek thee as my choicest, and my

Omne bonum in summo bono.

my chiefest good. God is *Alpha*, the fountain from whence all grace springs, and *Omega*, the Sea, to which all glory runs, and therefore early and primarily to bee sought. God is a perfect good, a solid good (*id bonum perfectum dicitur, cui nil accedere, solidum, cui nil decedere potest. Lactantius*) that is a perfect good, to which nothing can bee added, that a solid, from which nothing can bee spared; such a good God is, and therefore early and chiefly to bee sought. God is a pure and simple good, hee is a light, in whom there is no darkness, a good, in whom there is no evil. The goodness of the Creature is mixt, yea, that little goodnesse that is in the Creature is mixt with much evil, but God is an immixt good, hee is good, hee is a pure good, hee is all over good, he is nothing but good. God is an All-sufficient good, *walk before mee, and be upright, I am God All-sufficient*, in the 17. of *Genesis*, and the 1 *verse*. *Habet omnia, qui*
habet

1 Joh. 1. 5

Quicquid est in Deo, est ipse Deus.

habet habentem omnia. Aug. Hee hath all, that hath the haver of all. God hath in himself all power to defend you, all wisdome to direct you, all mercy to pardon you, all grace to inrich you, all righteousnesse to cloathe you, all goodnes to supply you, and all happinesse to Crown you. God is a satisfying good, a good that fills the heart, and quiets the soul; in the 33. of *Genesis*, and the 11. *verse. I have enough*, saith good *Jacob, I have all*, saith *Jacob*, for so the Hebrew hath it (*Cholli*) I have all, I have all comforts, all delights, all contents, &c. In having nothing, I have all things, because I have Christ, having therefore all things in him, I seek no other reward, for *hee is the universal reward*, saith one. As the worth and value of many pecces of silver is to bee found in one peece of gold. So all the petty excellencies that are scattered abroad in the creatures, are to bee found in God, yea all the
whole

Cant. 2. 3

whole volume of perfections, which is spread through Heaven and Earth, is epitomized in him. No good, below him that is the greatest good, can satisfie the soul; a good wife, a good childe, a good name, a good estate, a good friend, cannot satisfie the soul; these may please, but they cannot satisfie. All abundance, if it bee not my God, is to mee nothing but poverty and want, said one.

Omnis copia quæ non est Deus meus, mihi egestas est. Aug. Soliloq. c. 13.

Ah! that young men and women would but in the morning of their youth, seek, yea, seek early, seek earnestly, seek affectionately, seek diligently, seek primarily, and seek unweariedly this God, who is the greatest good, the best good, the most desirable good; who is a suitable good, a pure good, a satisfying good, a total good, and an eternal good.

Why young persons should bee really good betimes.

Reason IX.

Because the time of youth is the choicest and fittest time for service.
Now

Now your parts are lively, senses fresh, memory strong, and nature vigorous, the daies of your youth, are the spring and morning of your time, they are the first-born of your strength; therefore God requires your non-age, as well as your dotage, the Wine of your times, as well as the Lees, as you may see typified to you in the first fruits, which were dedicated to the Lord, and the first-born. The time of youth, is the time of salvation, it is the acceptable time, it is thy summer, thy harvest time. O young man! therefore do not sleep, but up and be doing, awaken thy heart, rouse up thy soul, and improve all thou hast, put out thy reason, thy strength, thy all, to the treasuring up of heavenly graces, precious promises, divine experiences, and spiritual comforts, against the Winter of old age, and then old age will not bee to thee an evil age, but as it was to *Abraham, a good old age*; do not put off God with fair

Marginalia:
The daies of youth are called, *ætas bona*, in *Cicero*, and *ætas optima*, in *Seneca*.

Exod. 13. 2.
Exod. 22. 9.

Gen. 25. 28.

fair promises, and large pretences, till your last sands are running, and the daies of dotage have overtaken you. That's a sad word of the Prophet, *Cursed bee the deceiver, which hath in his Flock a Male, and yet offereth to the Lord a corrupt thing.*

Ah young men and women, who are like the Almond Tree, you have many males in the Flock, your strength is a male in your Flock, your time is a male in the Flock, your reason is a male in the Flock, your parts are a male in the Flock, and your gifts are a male in the Flock; now if hee be curst that hath but one male in his Flock, and shall offer to God a corrupt thing, a thing of no worth, of no value, how will you bee curst, and curst? curst at home, and curst abroad, curst temporally, curst spiritually, and curst eternally, who have many males in your Flock, and yet deal so unworthily, so fraudulently, and false-heartedly with God, as to put him off with the dreggs of your

Mal. 1. 14.

Jer. 1. 11. The Almond tree blossomes in *January* (while it is yet winter) and the fruit is ripe in *March.*

and Excellency. 47

your time and strength, while you spend the Prim-rose of your youth, in the service of the world, the Flesh, and the Devil.

The Fig-tree in the Gospel, that did not bring forth fruit timely and seasonably, was curst to admiration; the time of youth is the time and season for bringing forth the fruits of Righteousness and Holiness, and if these fruits bee not brought forth in their season, you may justly fear, that the curses of Heaven will secretly and insensibly soak and sink into your souls, and then woe, woe to you that ever you were born; the best way to prevent this Hell of Hells, is to give God the cream and flower of your youth, your strength, your time, your talents; vessels that are betimes seasoned with the savour of life, never lose it, *Prov.* 22. 6.

Reason X.

Because death may suddenly and un-

Mat. 21. 20

Why young persons should bee really good, (in good earnest) betimes.

unexpectedly seize upon you, you have no lease of your lives.

Youth is as fickle as old age, the young man may finde graves enough of his length in burial places; as green wood, and old loggs meet in one fire, so young sinners and old sinners meet (in one hell) and burn together; when the young man is in his spring and prime, then hee is cut off, and dies; one dyeth in his full strength (or in the strength of his perfection, as the Hebrew hath it) being wholly at ease and quiet. His breasts are full of milk, and his bones are moistened with marrow. *Davids* children die, when young, so did *Jobs*, and *Jeroboams*, &c. Every daies experience tells us, that the young mans life is as much a vapour, as the old mans is.

I have read of an *Italian* Poet, who brings in a proper young man, rich and potent, discoursing with Death, in the habit of a Mower, with his Sythe in his hand,

Pares nascuntur, pares moriuntur, in the womb, and in the tomb they are all alike.
Job 21. 23, 24.
'Tis an allegorical description of the highest prosperity.

and Excellency.

hand, cutting down the life of man (*For all flesh is grass,* Isa. 40. 6.) and wilt thou not spare any mans person, saith the young man? I spare none, saith Death, mans life is but a day, a short day, a winters day, oft-times the Sun goes down upon a man, before it be well up; your day is short, your work is great, your journey long, and therefore you should rise early, and set forward towards Heaven betimes, as that man doth that hath a long journey to go in a winters day.

    The life of man is absolutely short. *Behold thou hast made my daies as an hands breadth.* The life of man is comparatively short, and that if you compare mans life now to what hee might have reacht, had hee continued in innocency. Sin brought in Death, Death is a fall, that came in by a fall; or if you compare mans life now, to what they did reach to before the Flood, then several lived, six, seven, eight, nine hundred

Marginal notes: Deaths motto is, *Nulli cedo,* I yield to none. Psal. 39. 5. Gen. 9.

The Young Mans Duty

Gen. 9.
Pſal. 39. 5

dred years; or if you compare mens daies with the daies of God, *Mine age is as nothing before thee*; or if you compare the daies of man, to the daies of Eternity.

The Heathen could ſay, that the whole life of man ſhould bee nothing elſe but (*Meditatio mortis*) a meditation of death.

Ah! Young Men, Young Men, can you ſeriouſly conſider of the brevity of mans life, and trifle away your time, the offers of grace, your precious ſouls, and eternity? &c. ſurely you cannot, ſurely you dare not; if you do but in good earneſt ponder upon the ſhortneſs of mans life. It is recorded of *Philip* King of *Macedon*, that hee gave a penſion to one, to come to him every day at dinner, and to cry to him (*memento te eſſe mortalem*) remember thou art but mortal.

Ah! young men and old had need bee often put in minde of their mortality, they are too apt to forget that day, yea, to put farre from them the thoughts of that day. I have read of three that could not endure to hear that bitter

ter word, death, mentioned in their ears, and surely this age is full of such monsters.

And as the life of man is very short, so it is very uncertain, now well, now sick, alive this hour, and dead the next. Death doth not alwaies give warning before hand, sometimes hee gives the mortal blow suddenly, hee comes behinde with his dart, and strikes a man at the heart, before hee saith, *have I found thee, O mine enemy?* Eutichus fell down dead suddenly, *Act.* 20.9. Death suddenly arrested *Davids* Sons, and *Jobs* Sons, *Augustus* died in a complement, *Galba* with a sentence, *Vespatian* with a jest, *Zeuxes* dyed laughing at the picture of an old woman, which hee drew with his own hand, *Sophocles* was choaked with the stone in a Grape, *Diodorus* the Logician died for shame, that hee could not answer a jocular question propounded at the Table by *Stilpo*, *Joannes Measius*, preaching upon the raising of the woman

Petrarch telleth of one who being invited to dinner the next day, answered, *Ego à multis annis crastinum non habui.* I have not had a morrow for this many years.

of

of *Naims* Son from the dead, within three hours after died himself.

Ah! Young men and women, have you not cause, great cause to bee good betimes? for death is sudden in his approaches, nothing more sure than death, and nothing more uncertain than life; therefore know the Lord betimes, turn from your sins betimes, lay hold on the Lord, and make peace with him betimes, that you may never say, as *Cæsar Borgias* said, when hee was sick to death, when I lived (said hee) I provided for every thing but death, now I must die, and am unprovided to die, &c.

Reason XI.

Why young persons should bee really good betimes.

Because it is ten to one, nay, a hundred to ten, if ever they are converted, if they are not converted when they are young.

God

and Excellency. 53

God usually begins with such betimes, that hee hath had thoughts of love and mercy towards them from everlasting, the instances cited to prove the Doctrine, confirms this Argument; and if you look abroad in the world, you shall hardly finde one Saint among a thousand, but dates his conversion from the time of his Youth. 'Twas the young ones that got through the wildernefs into *Canaan*. If the Tree do not bud, and blossome, and bring forth fruit in the Spring, it is commonly dead all the year after; if in the spring, and morning of your daies, you do not bring forth fruit to God, it is an hundred to one, that ever you bring forth fruit to him, when the evil daies of old age shall overtake you, wherein you shall say, you have no pleasure. For as the Son of *Syrach* observes, if thou hast gathered nothing in thy youth, what canst thou finde in thy age? tis rare, very rare, that God sows and reaps

Hos. 11. 1
When *Israel* was a childe, then I loved him, &c.

Numb. 26. 64.
An Hebrew Doctor observes, that of those six hundred thousand that went out of *Egypt*, there were but two persons that entered *Canaan*. Eccl. 25. 5

E 3   in

in old age, usually God sows the seed of grace in youth, that yeelds the harvest of joy in age.

Though true repentance bee never too late; yet late Repentance is seldome true. Millions are now in Hell, who have pleased themselves with the thoughts of after Repentance. The Lord hath made a promise to late repentance, but where hath hee made a promise of late repentance? yea, what can bee more just and equal, that such should seek, and not finde, who might have found, but would not seek; and that he should shut his ears against their late prayers, who have stopt their ears against his early calls? The Antient warriours would not accept an old man into their Army, as being unfit for service, and dost thou think that God will accept of thy dry bones, when Satan hath suckt out all the Marrow? What Lord, what Master, will take such into their service, who have all their daies served their enemies?

Prov. 1. 24--32.

enemies? and will God? will God? The *Circassians* (a kinde of Mongrel Christians) are said to divide their life betwixt sin and devotion, dedicating their youth to rapine, and their old age to repentance; if this bee thy case, I would not bee in thy case for ten thousand worlds.

Breerw. Enqui.

I have read of a certain great man, that was admonished in his sickness to repent, who answered, that hee would not repent yet, for if hee should recover, his companions would laugh at him; but growing sicker and sicker, his friends pressed him again to repent, but then hee told them, that it was too late (*Quia jam judicatus sum, & condemnatus*) for now said hee, I am judged and condemned.

Beda hath this story.

Reason XII.

Because else they will never attain to the honour of being old Disciples.

Why young men should bee really good betimes.

CHAP. II.

It is a very great honour to bee an Old Disciple.

NOw this honour none reach to, but such as are converted betimes, but such as turn to the Lord in the spring and morning of their youth: It is no honour for an old man to bee in coats, nor for an old man to bee a babe in grace. An A. B. C. old man is a sad and shameful sight: O but it is a mighty honour to bee a man when hee is old, that hee can date his conversion from the morning of his youth. Now that it is an honour to bee an old Disciple, I shall prove by an induction of particulars: As

Particular I.

All men will honour an old Disciple, Prov. 16. 31. *The hoary head is a Crown of glory, if it be found in the way of Righteausness.* God requires that the aged should bee honoured, Lev.

Marginal notes:

What more ridiculous than (*puer centum annorum*) a childe of an hundred years old?

A Crown is a very glorious thing, but there are but few of them.

an Old Disciple. 57

Lev. 19. 32. Thou shalt rise up before the hoary head, and honour the face of the old man (the old man here, is by some expounded the wise man) *and fear thy God, I am the Lord.* Hoariness is onely honourable, when found in a way of righteousness; a white head accompanied with a holy heart, makes a man truly honourable. There are two glorious sights in the world, the one is, a young man walking in his uprightnesse; and the other is, an old man walking in waies of righteousness; 'twas *Abrahams* honour, that hee went to his grave in a good old age, or rather as the Hebrew hath it, with a good gray head; many there bee that goe to their graves with a gray head; but this was *Abrahams* Crown, that hee went to his grave with a good gray head; had *Abrahams* head been never so gray, if it had not been good, it would have been no honour to him; a hoary head, when coupled with an unsanctified heart, is rather a curse, than a blessing,

Gen. 25. 8

sing, when the head is as white as Snow, and the soul as black as hell; God usually gives up such to the greatest scorn and contempt. Princes are hanged up by their hands, the faces of Elders were not honored, and this God had threatned long before. *The Lord shall bring against thee a Nation from far, a Nation of fierce countenance, which shall not regard the person of the old, nor shew favour to the young.*

I have read of *Cleanthes*, who was wont sometimes to chide himself: *Ariston* wondring thereat, asked him, whom chidest thou? *Cleanthes* laughed, and answered, I chide an old fellow (*qui canos quidem habet, sed mentem non habet*) who hath gray hairs indeed, but wants understanding, and prudence worthy of them. The Application I will leave to the gray heads, and gray beards of our time, who have little else to commend them to the world, but their hoary heads, and snowy beards.

Parti-

Marginal references: Isa. 65.20 · Lam. 5.12 · Deut. 28. 49, 50.

Particular II.

God usually reveals himself most to old Disciples, to old Saints, Job 12. 12. *With the Antient is wisdome, and in length of daies understanding.* God usually manifests most of himself to aged Saints, they usually pray most, and pay most, they labour most, and long most after the choicest manifestations of himself, and of his grace; and therefore he opens his bosome most to them, and makes them of his Cabinet-Council, *Gen.* 18. 17, 19. *And the Lord said, shall I hide from* Abraham *that thing which I do, for I know him, that hee will command his children, and his household after him, and they shall keep the way of the Lord, to do justice and judgement, that the Lord may bring upon* Abraham *that which hee hath spoken of him.* Abraham was an old friend; and therefore God makes him both of his Court and Council; wee usually open our hearts most freely, fully, and familiarly,

to

בישישים In the antient is wisdome. *Valentianius* the Emperors motto was *amicus veterimus optimus*) an old friend is best.

60 *It is an Honour to be*

to old friends. So doth God to his antient friends. Ah what a blessed sight and enjoyment of Christ had old *Simeon*, that made his very heart to dance in him! *Now Lord lettest thou thy servant depart in peace, according to thy word, for mine eies have seen thy salvation, &c.* I have seen him, who is my light, my life, my love, my joy, my crown, my heaven, my all; therefore now let *thy servant depart in peace.* So *Anna*, when shee was fourscore and four years old, was so filled with the discoveries and injoyments of Christ, that she could not but declare what shee had tasted, felt, seen, heard, and received from the Lord: She was ripe, and ready to discover the fulnesse, sweetnesse, goodnesse, excellency, and glory of that Christ, whom shee had long loved, feared, and served. So *Paul* lived in the light, sight, and sweet enjoyments of Christ, when aged, in years, in grace. So, when had *John* that glorious vision of Christ among the

Luke 2. 25, 26, 27, 28

Verse 36, 37, 38.

Phil. 4. 5, 7, 9.

Rev. 1. 7. -- ult.

an Old Disciple. 61

the golden Candlesticks, and those discoveries and manifestations of the ruine of *Rome*, the fall of Antichrist, the casting the beast, and false Prophet into a lake of fire, the conquest of the Kingdomes of the world, by Christs bow and sword, the binding up of Satan, and the new *Jerusalem* coming down from God out of Heaven, but when hee was old, when he was aged in years and in grace? The Lord speaks many a secret in the ears of aged Saints, of old Christians, which young Christians are not acquainted with, as that phrase imports, 2 *Sam.* 7. 27. *Thou O Lord God of hosts, hast revealed to thy servant*, so you read it in your books, but in the Hebrew it is, Lord thou hast revealed this to the ear of thy servant. Some wonder how that word to the ear comes to bee left out in your books, in which indeed the Emphasis lies; wee will tell many things in an old friends ear, which wee will not acquaint young ones with. So doth God many times

גליתה את־אזן
Galitha ethozen.

whisper

whisper an old Disciple in the ear, and acquaints him with such things that hee hides from those that are of younger years. And by this you may see what an honour it is to be an old Disciple.

Particular III.

An old Disciple, an old Christian, hee hath got the art of serving God, the art of Religion, got the art of hearing, the art of praying, the art of meditating, the art of repenting, the art of beleeving, the art of damping his natural self, his sinful self, his Religious self.

All Trades have their mystery and difficulty; so hath the Trade of Christianity; young Christians usually bungle in religious works, but old Christians acquit themselves like workmen that need not bee ashamed. A young Carpenter gives more blows, and makes more chips, but an old Artist doth the most, and best work; a young Christian may make most noise in religious duties, but an old Christian

Heb. 5. 11, 12, 13, 14 Yet as Solon was not ashamed to say that in his old age he was a learner, so those that are the greatest Artists in Christianity, will confesse, that they are still but learners.

tian makes the best work. A young Musician may play more quick and nimble upon an instrument, than an old, but an old Musician hath more skill and judgement than a young: the application is easie; and by this you may also see, what an honour it is to bee an old Christian, &c.

Particular IV.

An old Disciple, an old Christian, is rich in spiritual experiences. O the experiences that hee hath of the waies of God, of the workings of God, of the word of God, of the love of God! O the divine stories that old Christians can tell of the power of the word, of the sweetness of the word, of the usefulness of the word! as a light to lead the soul, as a staff to support the soul, as a spur to quicken the soul, as an anchor to stay the soul, and as a cordial to comfort and strengthen the soul! O the stories that hee can tell you concerning the love of Christ, the blood of Christ, the offices

1 Joh. 2. 1

Psal. 119. 49, 50. Old men love to speak of antient things.

offices of Christ, the merits of Christ, the righteousness of Christ, the graces of Christ, and the influence of Christ. O the stories that an old Disciple can tell you of the indwellings of the spirit, of the operations of the spirit, of the teachings of the spirit, of the leadings of the spirit, of the sealings of the spirit, of the witnessings of the spirit, and of the comforts and joyes of the spirit! O the stories that an old Christian can tell you of the evil of sin, the bitterness of sin, the deceitfulness of sin, the prevalency of sin, and the happiness of conquest over sin! O the stories that hee can tell you of the snares of Satan, the devices of Satan, the temptations of Satan, the rage of Satan, the malice of Satan, the watchfulness of Satan, and the waies of triumphing over Satan! As an old Souldier can tell you of many battels, many scarrs, many wounds, many losses, and many victories, even to admiration: So an old Saint is able

to

an Old Disciple.

to tell you many divine stories, even to admiration.

Pliny writes of the Crocodile, that shee grows to her last day. So aged Saints, they grow rich in spiritual experiences to the last. An old Christian being once asked, if hee grew in goodness, answered, yea, doubtless I do, for God hath said, *The Righteous shall flourish like the Palm-tree* (now the Palm-tree never loseth his leaf, or fruit, saith *Pliny*) *hee shall grow like a Cedar in Lebanon. Those that bee planted in the house of the Lord, shall flourish in the Courts of our God; They shall still bring forth fruit in old age, they shall bee fat and flourishing.* A fellow to this promise *Isaiah* mentions, *Hearken unto mee, O house of Jacob, and all the remnant of the house of Israel, which are born by mee, from the belly, which are carried from the womb, and even to your old age; I am hee, and even to hoary hairs will I carry you; I have made, and I will bear, even I will carry, and will deliver you.*

Hos. 14. 5, 6, 7.

Psal. 92. 12, 13, 14.

Isa. 46. 3, 4.

F There

It is an Honour to be

Dan. 7. 9. 13. 22.

There is nothing more commendable in fulness of age, than fulness of knowledge and experience, nor nothing more honourable, than to see antient Christians very much acquainted with the Antient of daies.

It is a brave sight to see antient Christians, like the Almond-tree. Now the Almond-tree doth flourish, and is full of blossomes in the Winter of old age, for as *Pliny* tells us, the Almond-tree doth blossome in the month of *January*. Experiments in Religion are beyond notions and impressions; a sanctified heart is better than a silver tongue; no man so rich, so honourable, so happy, as the Old Disciple, that is rich in spiritual experiences; and yet there is no Christian so rich in his experiences, but hee would be richer.

The Lawyer.

As *Julianus* said, that when hee had one foot in the grave, hee would have the other in the school. So though an Old Disciple hath one foot in the grave, yet hee will have

have the other in Christs School, that hee may still bee treasuring up more and more divine experiments; and by this also you see, *What an honour it is to bee an Old Disciple, &c.*

Particular V.
An Old Disciple is very stout, couragious, firm, and fixt in his resolution.

An Old Christian is like a Pillar, a Rock, nothing can move him, nothing can shake him, what is suckt in in youth, will abide in old age; Old Souldiers are stout and couragious, nothing can daunt nor discourage them. When *Joshua* was an hundred and ten years old, O how couragious and resolute was hee! *And if it seem evil unto you, to serve the Lord, chuse you this day whom you will serve, whether the Gods that your Fathers served, that were on the other side of the flood, or the gods of the Amorites, in whose land yee dwell: but as for mee and my house, wee will serve the*

Psal. 44. 9. ult.

Josh. 24. 15, 29.

the Lord. *And it came to pass, after these things, that* Joshua *the Son of* Nun, *the servant of the Lord dyed, being an hundred and ten years old.*

Confidius, a Senator of *Rome*, told *Cæsar* boldly, that the Senators durst not come to counsel for fear of his Souldiers; hee replied, why then dost thou go to the Senate? hee answered, because my age takes away my fear.

Ah! none so couragious, none so divinely fearless, none so careless in evil daies, as antient Christians. An old Christian knows, that that good will do him no good, which is not made good by perseverance: his resolution is like that of *Gonsalvo*, who protested to his souldiers, shewing them *Naples*, that hee had rather dye one foot forwards, than to have his life secured for long by one foot of retreat. Shall such a man as I am flee, said undaunted *Nehemia*? hee will couragiously venture life and limb, rather than by one foot of

Neh.6.11

of retreat, discredit profession with the reproach of fearfulness. It was a brave magnanimous speech of *Luther*, when dangers from opposers did threaten him, and his associates; Come (saith hee) let us sing the forty sixth *Psalm*, and then let them do their worst.

When *Polycarpus* was fourscore and six years old, hee suffered Martyrdome couragiously, resolutely, and undauntedly.

When one of the antient Martyrs was very much threatned by his persecutors, hee replyed, there is nothing of things visible, nothing of things invisible, that I fear; I will stand to my profession of the name of Christ, and contend earnestly for the faith once delivered to the Saints, come on it what will.

Old Disciples, old Souldiers of Christ, they have the heart and courage of *Shammah*, one of *Davids* worthies, who stood and defended the field, when all the rest fled. The Hebrews call a young man

Aristotle, (though a Heathen) could say, that in some cases a man had better lose his life, than be cowardly. *Arist. Ethic.* 3. cap. 1.

2 Sam. 23. 11, 12.

Nagnar, which springs from a root that signifies to shake off, or to bee tossed to and fro, to note how fickle, and how constant in inconstancy young men are, they usually are persons, either of no resolution for good, or of weak resolution; they are too often wonne with a Nut, and lost with an Apple; but now, aged Christians, in all Earthquakes, they stand fast, like *Mount Zion*, that cannot bee removed. And by this also you may see, *what an honour it is to bee an Old Disciple*, an old Christian.

Mat. 19. 20, 21, 22.

Particular VI.

An old Disciple, an old Christian, is prepared for death, hee hath been long a dying to sin, to the world, to friends, to self, to relations, to all, and no man so prepared to dye, as hee that thus daily dies.

Rom. 6. 6 Gal. 5. 24. ch. 6. 14.

An old Disciple hath lived sincerely to Christ, hee hath lived eminently to Christ, hee hath lived in all conditions, and under all changes to Christ, hee hath lived exemplarily to Christ, he hath lived

Rom. 14. 7, 8. Phil. 2. 21, 22, 23.

ed long to Christ, and therefore the more prepared to die, and bee with Christ. An old Disciple hath a Crown in his eye, a Pardon in his bosome, and a Christ in his arms; and therefore may sweetly sing it out with old *Simeon*, *Lord, now let thy servant depart in peace*. As *Hillary* said to his soul, Soul, thou hast served Christ this seventy years, and art thou afraid of death? go out soul, go out.

Many a day said old *Cowper* have I sought death with tears, not out of impatience, distrust, or perturbation, but because I am weary of sin, and fearful to fall into it. *Nazianzen* calls upon the King of terrors, devour mee, devour mee. And *Austin*, when old, could say, shall I dye ever? yes, or shall I dye at all? yes, why then Lord, if ever, why not now? why not now? so when *Modestus*, the Emperors Lieutenant threatned to kill *Basil*, hee answered, if that bee all, I fear not; yea, your Master cannot more pleasure mee, than

Zeno, a wise Heathen, said, I have no fear, but of old age.

Cyprian could receive the cruellest sentence of death with a *Deo gratias*. God I thank thee in sending mee unto my heavenly Father, to whom I now live, and to whom I desire to hasten.

I cannot say, as hee (said old Mr. *Stephen Martial* a little before his death) I have not so lived, that I should now bee afraid to dye, but this I can say, I have so learned Christ, that I am not afraid to dye. Old Christians have made no more to dye, than to dine. It is nothing to dye when the Comforter stands by. Old Disciples know, that to die, is but to lye down in their beds, they know that their dying day is better than their birth day; and this made *Solomon* to prefer his Coffin before his Crown; the day of his dissolution, before the day of his coronation.

The Ancients were wont to call the daies of their death, *Natalia*, not dying daies, but birth daies.

The Jews to this day stick not to call their *Golgotha*'s *Batte Caiim*, the houses or places of the Living; Old Christians know, that

Isa. 57. 1, 2

Eccles. 7. 1

that death is but an entrance into life, 'tis but a passeover, a jubile, 'tis but the Lords Gentleman-usher, to conduct them to Heaven; and this prepares them to dye, and makes death more desirable than life; and by this you may see, that it is an honour to bee an Old Disciple.

Particular VII.

An Old Disciple, an Old Christian, shall have a great reward in Heaven.

Old Christians have done much, and suffered much for Christ; and the more any man doth, or suffers for Christ here, the more glory hee shall have hereafter. 'Twas the saying of an Old Disciple upon his dying bed, Hee is come, hee is come (meaning the Lord) with a great reward for a little work. *Agrippa* having suffered imprisonment for wishing *Caius* Emperor; the first thing *Caius* did when hee came to the Empire, was to prefer *Agrippa* to a Kingdome, he

1 Cor. 15. ult.
2 Cor. 9.6
Mat. 5. 10, 11, 12.
God will reward his Servants *Secundum laborem*, according to their labour, though not *Secundum proventum*, according to the successe of their labour.

hee gave him also a chain of Gold, as heavy as the chain of Iron that was upon him in prison; And will not Christ richly reward all his suffering Saints? Surely hee will: Christ will at last pay a Christian for every prayer hee hath made, for every Sermon hee hath heard, for every tear hee hath shed, for every morsel hee hath given, for every burden hee hath born, for every battel hee hath fought, for every enemy hee hath slain, and for every temptation that hee hath overcome.

Cyrus in a great expedition against his enemies, the better to incourage his souldiers to fight, in an oration that hee made at the head of his Army, promised upon the victory, to make every foot-souldier an horseman, and every horseman a Commander, and that no Officer that did valiantly, should bee unrewarded; but what are *Cyrus* his rewards, to the rewards that Christ our General, promises to his? *Rev. 3. 21. To him that overcometh*

Mat. 19. 28.
Luke 22. 30.
Mat. 5. 12

an Old Disciple. 75

vercometh, will I grant to sit with mee in my Throne, even as I also overcame, and am set down with my Father in his Throne. As there is no Lord to Christ, so there is no rewards to Christs, his rewards are the greatest rewards, hee gives Kingdomes, Crowns, Thrones, hee gives grace, and glory, *Psal.* 48. 11.

It is said of *Araunah*, that noble *Jebusite*, renowned for his bounty, that he had but a subjects purse, but a Kings heart: but Jesus Christ hath a Kings purse, as well as a Kings heart, and accordingly hee gives.

And as Christs rewards are the greatest rewards, so his rewards are the surest rewards; hee is faithful that hath promised, 1 *Thes.* 5. 24.

Antiochus promised often, but seldome gave (upon which hee was called in way of derision, a great promiser) but Jesus Christ never made any promise, but hee hath or will perform it, 2 *Cor.* 1. 20. nay, hee is often better than his word,
1 *Cor.*

As the King in Plutarch said of a groat, it is no Kingly gift, and of a Talent, it is no base bribe.

1 *Cor.* 2. 9. hee gives many times more than wee ask. The sick man of the Palsie asked but health, and Christ gave him health, and a pardon to boot. *Solomon* desired but wisdome, and the Lord gave him wisdome, and honour, and riches, and the favour of Creatures, as Paper and Pack-thred into the bargain. *Jacob* asked him but cloaths to wear, and bread to eat, and the Lord gave him these things, and riches, and other mercies into the bargain.

<small>Mat. 9. 2</small>

<small>2 Chr. 1. 10,11,12, 13,14, 15</small>

<small>Gen. 28. 20 compared with Gen. 32. 10.</small>

Christ doth not measure his gifts by our Petitions, but by his own Riches and Mercies. Gracious souls many times receive many gifts and favours from God, that they never dreamt of, nor durst presume to beg, which others extreamly strive after, and go without.

Archelaus being much importuned by a covetous Courtier for a cup of gold wherein hee drank, gave it unto *Euripides* that stood by, saying, Thou art worthy to ask,

ask, and bee denied, but *Euripides* is worthy of gifts, although he ask not.

The Prodigal craves no more but the place of a hired servant, but hee is entertained as a Son, hee is clad with the best robe, and fed with the fatted Calf, hee hath a Ring for his hand, and Shooes for his feet, rich supplies more than hee desired. *Jacobs* Sons in a time of famine, desired onely Corn, and they return with corn and money in their sacks, and with good news too, *Joseph* is alive, and governour of all *Egypt*. Luke 15. 19--25.

Gen. 42.

And as his rewards are greater and surer than others rewards, so they are more durable and lasting than others rewards; the Kingdome that hee gives, is a Kingdome that shakes not; the treasures that hee gives, are treasures that corrupt not; and the glory that hee gives, is glory that fadeth not away; but the rewards that men give, are like themselves, fickle and unconstant, they are withering and fading. Heb. 12. 28.
Mat. 6.19, 20.
1 Pet. 1.4

Xerxes

Xerxes crowned his steers-man in the morning, and beheaded him in the evening of the same day.

And *Andronicus* the Greek Emperor, crowned his Admiral in the morning, and then took off his head in the afternoon.

Roffensis had a Cardinals Hat sent him, but his head was cut off before it came to him. Most may say of their Crowns, as that King said of his, O Crown! more noble than happy. It was a just complaint which long ago was made against the Heathen gods, (*O faciles dare summa deos, eademque tueri difficiles!*) they could give their favourites great gifts, but they could not maintain them in the possession of them; the world may give you great things, but the World cannot maintain you in the possession of them; but the great things, the great rewards that Christ gives his, hee will for ever maintain them in the possession of them, otherwise Hea-

Heaven would not bee Heaven, Glory would not bee Glory: now by all thefe things you fee, that it is a very great honour to bee an old Difciple, an old Chriftian; and this honour you will never attain to, except you beginne to bee really good betimes, except in the morning of your youth, you return to the Lord, and get an intereft in him.

I fhall now come to make fome Ufe and Application of this weighty truth, to our felves.

You fee beloved, that it is the great Duty and Concernment of Young Men, *To bee really good betimes*: If this bee fo; Then,

Ufe I.

Firft, This Truth looks fowerly and fadly upon fuch young men, that are onely feemingly good, that make fome fhews of goodnefs, but are not right toward wards God at the root.

As *Joash* when hee was young, hee seemed to have good things in him towards the Lord, whilst good *Jehoiada* lived, but when *Jehoiada* was dead, *Joash* his goodness was buried with him.

Ah! how many in these daies that have been seemingly good, have turned to bee naught, very naught, yea, stark naught?

It is said of *Tiberius*, that whilst *Augustus* ruled, hee was no waies tainted in his reputation; and that whilst *Drusus* and *Germanicus* were alive, hee feigned those virtues which hee had not, to maintain a good opinion of himself, in the hearts of the people; but after hee had got himself out of the reach of contradiction and controulment, there was no fact in which hee was not faulty, no crime to which hee was not accessary.

Oh! That this were not applicable to many young persons

---

margin notes:

2 Chron. 24. 1, 2, 3, 4, 5, 6, 13, 14, 15, 16

Neroes first five years are famous, but afterwards who more cruel?

There are some that write, that after *Demas* had forsaken *Paul*, hee became a Priest in an Idol-Temple.

sons in these daies, who have made great shews, and taken upon them a great name, who have begun to outshine the Stars, but are now gone out like so many snuffs, to the dishonour of God, the reproach of the Gospel, the grief of others, and the hazard of their own souls.

It was a custome of old, when any was baptized, the Minister delivered a white garment to bee put on, saying, Take thou this white vestment, and see thou bring it forth without spot at the judgement seat of Jesus Christ; whereupon one *Maritta* baptizing one *Elpidophorus*, who when hee was grown up, proved a prophane wretch, hee brings forth the white garment, and holding it up, shakes it against him, saying, This linnen garment *Elpidophorus* shall accuse thee at the coming of Christ, which I have kept by mee as a witness of thy Apostacy.

Ah! young men and women, your former professions will bee a sad witness against you in the great

Crabs that go backward, are reckoned among the unclean creatures. Lev. 11. 10

great day of our Lord Jesus, except you repent and return in good earnest to the Lord.

Oh it had been better that you had never made profession, that you had never set your faces towards Heaven, that you had never pretended to God and Christ, that you had never known the way of Righteousness, than after you have known it, to turn from the holy Commandement!

Cyprian in his Sermon *de lapsis*, reporteth of divers, who forsaking the Faith, were given over to evil spirits, and died fearfully.

Oh the delusions, and the Christ-dethroning, conscience-wasting, and soul-undoing opinions, and principles, that many young ones (who once were hopeful ones) are given up to! That dreadful Scripture seems to bee made good in power upon them: *All you that forsake the Lord, shall come to bee ashamed, and they that depart from him, shall bee written upon the dust*; to begin well, and not to proceed, is but

---

Prov. 14. 14

2 Pet. 2. 21.

Jer. 17. 13

The Vanity of Youth. 43

but to aspire to a higher pitch, that the fall may bee the more desperate. Backsliding is a wounding sin. You read of no arms for the back, though you do for the breast: Hee that is but seemingly good, will prove at last exceeding bad, 2 *Tim.* 3. 13. *They wax worse and worse, deceiving, and being deceived.*

Hos. 4. 14
Eph. 6. 11.
18.

The Wolf, though hee often dissembles, and closely hides his nature, yet hee will one time or other shew himself to bee a Wolf.

In the daies of *Hadrian* the Emperor, there was one *Bencosby*, who gathering a multitude of Jews together, called himself *Ben-cocuba*, the son of a star, applying that prophesy to himself, *Num.* 23. 17. but his mask was taken off, his Hypocrisy discovered, and hee found to be *Barchosaba*, the son of a lye; this age hath afforded many such Monsters, but their folly is discovered, and their practises abhorred. This was the young mans commendation in the Text, *That there was found in him some real*

Comets make a greater blaze than fixed stars.

G 2 *good*

good towards the Lord.

Use II.

2. This truth looks sowerly and sadly upon such young men, who are so far from having good things in them towards the Lord, that they give themselves up to those youthful lusts and vanities that are dishonouring, provoking, and displeasing to the Lord, who roar and revel, and gad, and game, and dice, and drink, and drab, and what not; these make work with a witness for repentance, or hell, or the physician of souls.

I shall but touch upon the evils of youth, and then come to that which is mostly intended.

CHAP. III.

The first evil that most properly attends youth, is Pride.

1 Tim. 3. 6

Pride of heart, pride of apparel, pride of parts; young men are apt to to bee proud of health, strength, friends, relations, wit, wealth, wisdome: two things are very rare, the one is to see a young man humble and watchful, and the other is to see an old man contented and chearful.

Bernard saith, that pride is the rich mans couzen, and experience every day speaks out pride to bee the young mans couzen. God (said one) had three Sons, *Lucifer*, *Adam*, and *Christ*, the first aspired to bee like God in power, and was therefore thrown down from Heaven: The second to bee like him in knowledge, and was therefore deservedly driven out of *Eden*, when young: The third did altogether imitate and follow him in his goodness, mercy and humility, and by so doing obtained an everlasting inheritance.

Remember this young men, and as you would get a Paradise, and keep a Paradise, get humble, and keep humble. Pride is an evil that puts men upon all manner of evil

Pride cannot climb so high, but justice will sit above.

vii. *Accius* the Poet, though he were a dwarf, yet would be pictured tall of stature.

Psaphon, a proud Lybian, would needs bee a God, and having caught some birds, hee taught them to speak and prattle, The great god *Psaphon*.

Menecrates, a proud Physician, wrote thus to King *Philip*, *Menecrates* a God, to *Philip* a King.

Proud *Simon* in *Lucian*, having got a little wealth, changed his name (from *Simon* to *Simonides*) for that there were so many beggers of his kin, and set the house on fire wherein hee was born, because no body should point at it.

What sad evils *Pharaohs* pride, and *Hamans* pride, and *Herods* pride, and *Belshazzars* pride, put them upon, I shall not now mention.

Acco, an old woman, seeing her deformity in a glass, went mad, &c.

Ah young men, young men! had others a window to look into your breasts, or did your hearts stand where your faces do, you would even bee afraid of your selves,

selves, you would loathe and abhor your selves.

Ah! young men, young men, as you would have God to keep house with you, as you would have his minde and secrets made known to you, as you would have Christ to delight in you, and the Spirit to dwell in you, as you would be honoured among Saints, and attended, and guarded by Angels, get humble, and keep humble.

Tertullians counsel to the young gallants of those times, was excellent, cloathe your selves (said he) with the silk of piety, with the sattin of sanctity, and with the purple of modesty: So shall you have God himself to be your Suter.

Tert. de Cult. fæm. Cap. 13.

2 Evil.

The second evil that youth is subject to, is sensual pleasures and delights. Rejoyce, *O young man, in thy youth, and let thy heart chear thee in the daies of thy youth, and walk in the waies of thy heart, and in the sight of thine eies.* The wise man by an Ironical concession bids him

Eccl. 11.9
2 Sam. 13
23 -- 29.
ἡδονὴ δέλεαρ κακῶν.
Pleasure is the bait of sin, saith Plato.

him rejoyce, &c. Sin,&c. thou art wilful, and resolved upon taking thy pleasure, go on, take thy course, this hee speaks by way of mockage, and bitter scoffe, &c. but know thou, that for all thee things God will bring thee into judgement. So *Sampson* made a feast; for so used the young men to do, the hearts of young men usually are much given up to pleasure. I have read of a young man, who was very much given up to pleasures, hee standing by St. *Ambrose*, and seeing his excellent death, turned to other young men by him, and said,

Oh! that I might live with you, and dye with him. Sensual pleasures are like to those Locusts, *Rev.* 9.7. the crowns upon whose heads, are said to be only as it were such, or such in appearance, and like gold, but *vers.* 10. it is said, there were (not as it were, but) stings in their tails.

Sensual pleasures, are but seeming, and appearing pleasures, but the pains that attend them are

Marginal notes:
Judg. 14. 10.

They were much out that held pleasure to be mans *summum bonum*.

The Vanity of Youth. 89

true and real; hee that delights in sensual pleasures, shall finde his greatest pleasures, become his bitterest pains.

The Heathens look'd upon the back parts of pleasure, and saw it going away from them, and leaving a sting behinde.

Pleasures pass away as soon as they have wearied out the body, and leave it as a bunch of grapes, whose juice hath been pressed out; which made one to say (*Nulla major voluptas, quam voluptatis fastidium*) I see no greater pleasure in this world, than the contempt of pleasure.

Julian, though an Apostate, yet professed, that the pleasures of the body were far below a great spirit. And *Tully* saith, hee is not worthy of the name of man (*qui unum diem velit esse in voluptate*) that would entirely spend one whole day in pleasures; it is better not to desire pleasures, than to enjoy them. I said of laughter, it is mad, and of mirth, what dost

Eccl. 2. 2.

dost thou? The interrogation bids a challenge to all the Masters of mirth, to produce any one satisfactory fruit which it affordeth, if they could.

Xerxes being weary of all pleasures, promised rewards to the inventers of new pleasures, which being invented, hee neverthelefs remained unsatisfied. As a Bee flieth from flower to flower, and is not satisfied, and as a sick man removes from one bed to another, from one seat to another, from one chamber to another, for ease, and finds none: So men given up to sensual pleasures, go from one pleasure to another, but can finde no content, no satisfaction in their pleasures. *The eye is not satisfied with seeing, nor the ear filled with hearing.* There is a curse of unsatisfiablenefs lies upon the creature; honours cannot satisfie the ambitious man, nor riches the covetous man, nor pleasures the voluptuous man; man cannot take off the wearinefs of one pleasure by

Eccl. 1. 8.

The Vanity of Youth.

by another, for after a few evaporated minutes are spent in pleasures, the body presently fails the mind, and the mind the desire, and the desire the satisfaction, and all the man.

Pleasures are *Junos* in the pursute, and but clouds in the enjoyment; Pleasure is a beautiful harlot, sitting in her chariot, whose four wheels are Pride, Gluttony, Lust, and Idleness; the two horses are prosperity and abundance, the two drivers are Idleness and Security, her attendants and followers are guilt, grief, late repentance (if any) and oft death and ruine; many great men, and many strong men, and many rich men, and many hopeful men, and many young men, have come to their ends by her; but never any enjoyed full satisfaction and content in her.

Ah! Young men, Young men, avoid this harlot, and come not neer the door of her house. And as for lawful pleasures, let mee onely say this, 'tis your wisdome onely

Beeanus saith, that the fruit of the tree of knowledge is sweet, but in the end it breeds *choler*, so do worldly pleasures.

onely to touch them, to taste them, and to use them, as *Mithridates* used poison, to fortifie your selves against casual extremities and maladies: when Mr. *Roger Ascham* asked the Lady *Jane Grey*, how shee could lose such pastime, her Father with the Dutchess, being a hunting in the Park, smilingly answered, all the sport in the Park is but a shadow of that pleasure I finde in this book, having a good book in her hand.

Augustine before his conversion, could not tell how to live without those pleasures which hee delighted much in, but when his nature was changed, and his heart graciously turned to the Lord, O how sweet (saith hee) is it to be without those former sweet delights!

Ah! Young men, when once you come to experience the goodnesse and sweetnesse that is in the Lord, and in his word and waies, you will then sit down and grieve that you have spent more Wine in the cup, than Oil in the lamp.

There

The Vanity of Youth.

There are no pleasures so delighting, so satisfying, so ravishing, so ingaging, and so abiding, as those that spring from union, and communion with God; as those that flow from a sense of interest in God, and from an humble and a holy walking with God.

3 Evil.

The third sin of youth is rashnesse.

They many times know little, and fear less, and so are apt rashly to run on, and run out often to their hurt, but more often to their hazard. *Exhort young men to bee sober minded, or discreet.* They are apt to bee rash, to bee hot-spurs. As you may see in *Rehoboams* young Counsellers, who counselled him to tell the people (that groaned under their burdens) that his little finger should bee thicker than his Fathers loins, and that hee would add to their yoak, and that
where-

Arist. Polit.

Tit. 2. 6.

1 Kings 12. 8, 9, 10, 11.

whereas his Father had chastized them with Whips, hee would chastize them with Scorpions, this rash counsel proved *Rehoboams* ruine; yea, *David* himself, though a good man, yet being in his warm blood, and young, how sadly was hee overtaken with rashness? *As the Lord God of Israel liveth* (saith hee) *except thou hadst hastened, and come to meet mee, surely there had not been left unto* Nabal, *by to morrow light, any that pisseth against the wall.* And this hee bindes with an oath; because the Master was foolishly wilful, the innocent servants must all bee woful; And because *Nabal* had been niggardly of his bread, *David* would bee prodigal of his blood.

Ah! how unlike a Christian, yea, how below a man doth *David* carry it, when his blood is up, and hee a captive to rashnesse, and passion? Rashnesse will admit of naught for reason, but what unreasonable self shall dictate for reason; as sloath seldome

marginalia:
1 Sam. 25. 34, 35.
Diis proximus ille est, quem ratio, non ira, movet. Sen.
Hee is next to God, whom reason, not anger moveth.

dome bringeth actions to good birth, so rashness makes them alwaies abortive, ere well formed: A rash spirit is an ungodlike spirit; a rash spirit is a weak spirit, it is an effeminate spirit. *A man of understanding is of an excellent spirit*, or as the Hebrew will bear, is of a cool spirit, not rash and hot, ready at every turn to put out his soul in wrath. Rashness unmans a man, it will put a man upon things below man-hood. *Herostratus* (a hot-spur) an obscure base fellow, did in one night by fire destroy the Temple of *Diana* at *Ephesus*, which was two hundred and twenty years in building, of all *Asia*, at the cost of so many Princes, and beautified with the labours & cunning of so many excellent workmen; the truth is, there would bee no end, should I discover the many sad and great evils that are ushered into the world by that one evil, rashness, which usually attends youth, &c. and therefore young men decline it, and arm your selves against *it*, &c. 4 Evil.

Prov. 17. 27

4 Evil.

The fourth sin that ordinarily attends on youth, is mocking, and scoffing at religious men, and religious things.

They were young ones, that scoffingly and scornfully said to the Prophet, *Go up thou bald-head, Go up thou bald-head.* And the young men derided and mocked *Job. But now, they that are younger than I, have mee in derision; whose Fathers I would have disdained, to have set with the dogs of my flock. Upon my right hand rise the youth, they push away my feet, and they raise up against mee the waies of their destruction, &c.* And Oh that this age did not afford many such Monsters, who are notable, who are infamous in this black Art of scoffing and deriding the people of God, and the waies of God.

The *Athenians* once scoffed at *Sylla*'s wife, and it had well nigh cost the rasing of their City, hee
was

2 Kings 2. 23, 24.
Job 30. 1. 12, 13, 14, 15.

was so provoked with the indignity, and will you think it safe to scoffe at the people of God, who are the Spouse of Christ, who are as the apple of his eye, who are the signet on his right hand, his portion, his pleasant portion, his inheritance, his Jewels, his royal Diadem? Ah young men, young men! will you seriously consider how sadly and sorely hee hath punished other scoffers and mockers? and by his judgements on them, be warned never to scoff at the people of God, or his waies more. *Julian* the Emperour was a great scoffer of Christians, but at last hee was struck with an arrow from Heaven, that made him cry out (*vicisti Galilee*) thou *Galilean* (meaning our Saviour Christ) hast overcome mee. *Felix* for one malicious scoffe, did nothing day and night but vomit blood, till his unhappy soul was separated from his wretched body. *Pherecydes* was consumed by Worms alive, for giving

Rev. 21 --.
Zach. 2. 5.
Deut. 32. 9
Isa. 19. 25
Joel 2. 17
Psa. 33. 12
Isa. 62. 3

H Reli-

Religion but a nick-name. *Lucian*, for barking against Religion like a Dog, was by the just judgement of God devoured of Dogs. Remember these dreadful judgements of God on scoffers, and if you like them, then mock on, scoff on, but know, that justice will at last bee even with you, nay above you.

5. Evil.

The fifth and last Evil (that I shall mention) *that attends and waits on youth, is lustfulness, and wantonness.*

2 Tim. 2. 12.

Which occasioned aged *Paul* to caution his young *Timothy*, to flee youthful lusts. *Timothy* was a chaste and chastened peece, hee was much sanctified and mortified, his graces were high, and corruptions low; hee walked up and down this world, with dying thoughts, and with a weak, distempered, declining, dying body; his heart was in Heaven, and his foot in the Grave, and yet youth is such a slippery age, that *Paul* commands him

The Vanity of Youth.

him to flee, to post from youthful lusts; though *Timothy* was a good man, a weak sickly man, a marvellous temperate man, drinking water rather than wine, yet he was but a man, yea a young man; and therefore *Pauls* counsel and command is, that he flee youthful lusts. And *Solomon*, who had sadly experienced the slipperiness of youth, gives this counsel, *Put away the evils of thy flesh, for childhood and youth are vanity.* Hee was a young man that followed the Harlot to her house; hee was young in years, and young in knowledge; (*Salazar* upon the words saith) that was a happy age, that afforded but one simple young man among many, whereas late times afford greater store. Ah! too many of the youths of this age, instead of flying from youthful lusts, they post and pursue after youthful lusts.

Chrysostome speaking of youth, saith, it is (*difficilem, factibilem, fallibilem, vehementissimísq; egenem frænu*) hard to bee ruled, easie to

Eccl. 11. 10.

Prov. 7. 7, 8, 9, 10, 11, &c.

Chrysost. Homil. 1. *Ad populum.*

bee drawn away, apt to bee deceived, and standing in need of very violent reins.

Lapide. The Antients did picture youth like a young man naked, with a veil over his face; his right hand bound behinde him, his left hand loose, and Time behinde him pulling one threed out of his veil every day, intimating that young men are void of knowledge, and blind, unfit to do good, ready to do evil, till Time by little and little make them wiser. Well young man, remember this, that the least sparklings and kindlings of lusts, will first or last cost thee groans, & griefs, tears, and terrours enough. These five are the sins that usually are waiting and attending on youth, but from these the young man in the Text was by Grace preserved, and secured, which is more than I dare affirm of all, into whose hand this Treatise shall fall. But though these five are the sins of youth; yet they are not all the sins of youth, for youth is capable

The Vanity of Youth.

pable of, and subject to all other sins whatsoever, but these are the special sins that most usually waits and attends on young men, when they are in the spring and morning of their youth.

CHAP. IV.

I shall now hasten to the main Use that I intend to stand upon, and that is an Use of Exhortation, to all young persons.

Ah Sirs! as you tender the glory of God, the good of your bodies, the joy of your Christian friends, and the salvation of your own souls; bee exhorted and perswaded to bee really good betimes. It was the praise and honour of *Abijah*, that there was found in him some good thing towards the Lord in the Primrose of his child-hood.

Oh that it might be your honour and happiness! to bee really good betimes, that it might be to you a praise, and a name, that in the

Other sins attend youth, as 1 Ignorance. 1 Cor. 14. 20. 2 Falshood. Psa. 58.3. 3 Excessive love of liberty. 4 Impatience of Councils and reproofs. Jer. 31.18, 19. 5 Impudence. Isa. 3.5. 6 A trifling spirit, Eccles. 11. 10. 7 Prodigality. Use.

morn-

morning of your youth you have begun to seek the Lord, and to know and love the Lord, and to get an interest and propriety in the Lord: Now that this Exhortation may stick and take,

I beseech you seriously to weigh and ponder these following Motives, or Considerations.

1 Motive.

First consider, *It is an honour to bee good betimes.* A young Saint is like the morning star; hee is like a Pearl in a gold Ring. It is mentioned as a singular honour to the beleeving Jews, that they first trusted in Christ, that wee should bee to the praise of his glory, who first trusted in Christ, this was their praise, their crown, that they were first converted, and turned to Christ, and Christianity. So *Paul* mentioning *Andronicus* and *Junia*, doth not omit this circumstance of praise and honour, that they were in Christ before him. Salute *Andronicus* and *Junia* my Kinsmen and my fellow prisoners,

Eph. 1.12

Rom. 16.7

who

who are of note among the A-
postles, who also were in Christ before mee.

And so it was the honour of the
house of *Stephanas*, that they were | 1 Cor. 16. 15
the first fruits of *Achaia*, it was
their glory, that they were the first
that received and welcomed the
Gospel in *Achaia*. 'Tis a greater
honour for a young man to out-
wrastle sin, Satan, temptation, the
world, and lust, than ever *Alexander* the Great could attain unto. It
was *Judah* his praise and honour, | 2 Sam. 19. 15
that they were first in fetching
home *David* their King.

Ah! young men and women,
it will bee your eternal praise
and honour, if you shall bee before
others, if you shall bee the first
among many, who shall know
the Lord, and seek the Lord,
who shall receive the Lord, and
imbrace him; who shall cleave to
the Lord, and serve him; who shall
honour the Lord, and obey him;
who shall delight in the Lord, and
walk with him. The *Romans* built

H 4 Virtues

Virtues and Honours Temple close together, to shew, that the way to honour was by virtue, and indeed there is no Crown to that which goodness sets upon a mans head, all other honour is fading and withering. *Adonibezeck* a mighty Prince, is suddenly made fellow-commoner with the Dogs. And *Nebuchadnezzar* a mighty Conqueror, turned a grazing among the Oxen. And *Herod* reduced from a conceited god, to be the most loathsome of men, living carrion, arrested by the vilest of creatures, upon the suit of his affronted Creatour. And *Haman* feasted with the King one day, and made a feast for Crows the next. I might tell you of *Bajazet*, and *Belisarius*, two of the greatest Commanders in the world, and many others, who have suddenly fallen from the top of worldly honor and felicity, into the greatest contempt and misery, but I shall not at this time: But that honour that arises from mens being

Judg. 1. 7

Dan. 4. 28

Act. 12. 23

Esth. 7. 10

Young Men.

ing gracious betimes, is such honour, that the World can neither give nor take; it is honour, it is a Crown that will still bee green and flourishing, it is honour that will bed and board with a man, that will abide with a man under all tryals and changes, that will to the grave, that will to Heaven with a man.

Ah Sirs! It is no small honour to you, who are in the spring and morning of your daies, that the Lord hath left upon record several instances of his love and delight in young men, hee chose *David* a younger Brother, and passes by his elder Brothers; hee frowns upon *Esau*, and passes by his door, and sets his love and delight upon *Jacob* the younger Brother; hee kindly and lovingly accepts of *Abels* person and Sacrifice, and rejects both *Cains* person and Sacrifice, though hee was the elder Brother. Among all the Disciples, *John* was the youngest, and the most and best be-

1 Sam. 16. 11, 12, 13

Rom. 9. 12, 13

Gen. 4. 3, 4, 5, 6

Joh. 13. 23

beloved. There was but one young man that came to Christ, and hee came not aright; and all the good that was in him, was but some moral good, and yet Christ loved him, with a love of pitty and compassion; the Greek word signifies, to speak friendly, and deal gently with one; and so did Christ with him, all which should exceedingly encourage young men to bee good betimes, to bee gracious in the morning of their youth; no way to true honour like this, but

2 Motive.

Secondly, Consider, *Christ loved poor sinners, and gave himself for them; when he was in the prime of his age* (being supposed to be about thirty and three) *and will you put him off with the worst of your time?*

Ah! Young men, young men, Christ gave himself up to death, he made himself an offering for your sins, for your sakes, when hee was in the prime and flower of his age, and why then should you put off Christ

Marginalia:
Mark 10. 19, 20, 21

ἀγαπᾶν.

The sacrifices in the Law were young Lambs, and young Kids, to shew, that Christ our Sacrifice, should dye and suffer for our sins, in the flower of his age.

Young Men.

Christ to old age? Did hee dye for sin in the prime of his age? and will not you dye to sin in the prime of your age? Did hee offer himself for you in the spring and morning of his years? and will not you offer up your selves to him in the spring and morning of your years? O give not Christ cause to say, I dyed for you betimes, but you have not lived to mee betimes; I was early in my suffering for you, but you have not been early in your returning to mee; I made haste to compleat your Redemption, but you have made no haste to make sure your Vocation, and Election; I stayed not, I lingred not, but soon suffered what I was to suffer, and quickly did what was to bee done for your eternal welfare, but you have stayed and lingered (like *Lot* in *Sodome*) and have not done what you might have done in order to your everlasting good: in the Primerose of my daies, I sweat for you,

Rom. 12. 1, 2.

2 Pet. 1. 10

Gen. 19. 16

you, I wept for you, I bled for you, I hung on the cross for you, I bore the wrath of my Father for you, but you have not in the primrose of your daies sweat under the sense of divine displeasure, nor wept over your sins, nor mourned over mee, whom you have so often grieved and pierced; I could not be quiet nor satisfied till I had put you into a capacity, into a possibility of salvation, and yet you are well enough quieted and satisfied, though you do not know whether ever you shall bee saved.

Zach. 12. 10

Ah Sirs! how sad would it bee with you, if Jesus Christ should secretly thus expostulate with your consciences in this your day.

Oh! how terrible would it bee with you, if Christ should thus visibly plead against you in his great day. Ah! Young men, young men and women, who, but souls much left of God, blinded by Satan, and hardened in sin, can hear Jesus Christ speaking

2 Cor. 4. 3, 4

ing thus to them? I suffered for Sinners betimes, I laid down a ransome for souls betimes, I pacified my Fathers wrath betimes, I satisfied my Fathers justice betimes, I merited grace and mercy for sinners betimes, I brought in an everlasting righteousness upon the world betimes, &c. I say, who can hear Jesus Christ speaking thus, and his heart not fall in love and league with Christ, and his soul not unite to Christ, and resign to Christ, and cleave to Christ, and for ever bee one with Christ, except it bee such that are for ever left by Christ? Well, remember this (*Quanto pro nobis vilior, tanto nobis charior*) the more vilde Christ made himself for us, the more dear hee ought to bee unto us.

Ah! Young men, remember this, when Christ was young, hee was tempted and tried, when hee was in the morning of his daies, his wounds were deep, his burden weighty, his cup bitter, his sweat
pain-

Nolo vivere sine vulnere, cum te video vulneratum. Bonaventur. Oh my God, as long as I see thy wounds, I will never live without wounds.

Aut Deus naturæ patitur, aut mundi machina dissolvitur, said *Dionysius Alexandrinus.* Either the God of Nature suffered, or the frame of the world will bee dissolved.

painfull, his agony and torment, above conception, beyond expression; when hee was young, that blessed head of his was crowned with thorns, and those eyes of his that were purer than the Sun, were put out by the darknesse of death, and those ears of his which now hear nothing but *Hallelujahs* of Saints and Angels, were filled with the blasphemies of the multitude, and that blessed beautifull face of his, which was fairer than the Sons of men, was spit on by beastly filthy wretches, and that gracious mouth and tongue that spake as never man spake, was slandered and accused of blasphemy, and those hands of his which healed the sick, which gave out pardons, which swayed a Scepter in Heaven, and another on Earth, were nailed to the Cross, and those feet that were beautifull upon the Mountains, that brought the glad tydings of peace and salvation into the world, and that were like unto fine brass, were

Young Men.

were also nailed to the Cross; All these great and sad things did Jesus Christ suffer for you, in the prime and flower of his daies, and Oh! what an unspeakable provocation should this bee to all young ones, to give up themselves betimes to Christ, to serve, love, honour, and obey him betimes, even in the spring and morning of their youth.

Let the thoughts of a crucified Christ (saith one) bee never out of your mind; let them bee meat and drink unto you; let them be your sweetness and consolation, your honey and your desire, your reading and your meditation, your life, death, and resurrection.

3 Motive.

The third Motive or Consideration to provoke you to begin to be good betimes, in this, viz.

That it is the best and choicest way in the world, to bee rich in gracious experiences betimes,
(which

The Philosopher once said, solus sapiens dives, onely the wise man is the rich man.

(which are the best riches in all the world) as hee that sets up for himself betimes, is in the most hopeful way to bee rich betimes: So hee that is good in good earnest betimes, hee is in the ready way, the high-way of being rich in grace, and rich in goodness, they usually prove men of great observation, and great experience. God loves to shew these his beauty, and his glory in his Sanctuary. Hee delights to cause his glory and his goodnesse to pass before such: these shall finde all his paths drop marrow and fatnesse, for these the Lord of Hosts will make a feast of fat things, a feast of Wines on the Lees, of fat things full of marrow, of Wines on the Lees well refined; these shall have all manner of pleasant fruits laid up at their gates for their well beloved; none have so many choice pledges of Chrifts love, nor so many sweet kisses of Chrifts mouth, nor so many imbraces in Chrifts arms, as those souls that are good be-

Marginalia: Psal. 63. 1, 2. Exod. 3. 3. 19, 22, &c. Psal. 65. 11, 12. Isa. 25. 6. Can. 7. 13

Young Men. 113

betimes; O the grace, the goodness, the sweetness, the fatness that Christ is still a droping into their hearts! Christ will make their hearts his largest treasury, hee'l lay up most of his heavenly treasure in their souls; there hee will store up mercies new and old; there hee will treasure up all plenty, rariety and variety, there hee will lay up all that heart can wish, or need require; O the many drops of myrrhe that falls from Christs fingers upon their hearts! O the many secrets that Christ reveals in their ears! O the many Love-Letters that Christ sends to these! O the many visits that hee gives to these! O the turns, the walks, that hee hath in Paradise with these! there are none in the world for experience and intelligence to these. Ah! Young men, young men, as you would bee rich in the best riches, beginne to bee good betimes; as there is no Riches to spiritual Riches, so there is no

Earthly riches are full of poverty. Divitiæ corporales paupertatis plenæ sunt.

I way.

way to be rich in these riches, but by beginning to bee good (in good earnest) betimes.

As for worldly riches, Philosophers have contemned them, and preferred a contemplative life above them, and shall not Christians much more? the Prophet calls them *thick clay*, which will sooner break the back, than lighten the heart; they cannot better the soul, they cannot enrich the soul. Ah! how many thredbare souls are to bee found under silken cloaks and gowns, how often are worldly Riches like hang-men, they hide mens faces with a covering, that they may not see their own end, and then they hang them. And if they do not hang you, they will shortly leave you, they make themselves wings, and fly away; when one was a commending the Riches and Wealth of Merchants; I do not love that Wealth, said a Heathen, that hangs upon Ropes, if they break, the Ship miscarrieth, and

If there were any happiness in riches, the Gods would not want them saith Seneca.

and all is lost. Hee is rich enough (saith *Jerom*) that lacketh not bread, and high enough in dignity that is not forced to serve.

This worlds wealth that men so much desire
May well bee likened to a burning fire,
Whereof a little can do little harm,
But profit much our bodies well to warm
But take too much and surely thou shalt burn
So too much wealth, to too much woe does
(*turn.*

It was an excellent saying of *Lewis* of *Bauyer*, Emperour of Germany (*hujusmodi comparandæ sunt opes quæ cum naufragio simul enatent*) such goods are worth getting and owning, as will not sink or wash away if a shipwrack happen, but will wade and swim out with us; wee see, such are the spiritual Riches that will attend those, who in the spring and morning of their youth, shall know the Lord, and serve the Lord; and get an interest in the Lord; and thus much for the third Motive.

I 2 The

4 Motive.

The fourth Motive to provoke young ones to bee really good betimes, is, to consider, that *The present time, the present day, is the onely season that you are sure of.*

Time past cannot bee recalled, and time to come cannot bee ascertained. *To day if you hear his voice, harden not your hearts.* Behold now is the acceptable time, now is the day of salvation; some there bee that trifle away their time, and fool away their souls, and their salvation; to prevent this, the Apostle beats upon the τό νῦν, the present opportunity, because if that bee once past, there is no recovering of it; therefore as the Mariner takes the first fair wind to sail; and as the Merchant takes his first opportunity of buying and selling; and as the Husbandman takes the first opportunity of sowing and reaping; so should young men take the present season, the present day (which is their day) to bee good towards the

Marginalia: Heb. 3. 15. 2 Cor. 6. 2. The whole Earth hangs on a point, so doth Heaven and Eternity on an inch of opportunity.

the Lord, to seek him, and serve him, and not to post off the present season, for they know not what another day, another hour, another moment may bring forth: that door of grace that is open to day, may bee shut to morrow; that golden Scepter of mercy that is held forth in the Gospel this day, may bee taken in the next day; that love that this hour is upon the bare knee, intreating and beseeching young men to break off their sins by repentance, to return to the Lord, to lay hold on his strength, and bee at peace with him may the next hour bee turned into wrath. *Isa.27.4,5*

Ah! the noble motions that have been lost, the good purposes that have withered, the immortal souls that have miscarried, by putting off the present season, the present day. *Paul* discoursing before *Felix* of Rightooufness, and Temperance, and Judgement to come, and in this discourse striking at two special vices *Act.24.25* ces that *Felix* was particularly guilty of, hee falls a trembling, and being upon the wrack to hear such Doctrine, hee bids *Paul* depart for that time, and hee would call for him at a convenient season; here *Felix* neglects his present season, and wee never read that ever after this hee found a convenient time or season to hear *Paul* make an end of the subject hee had begun! So Christ made a very fair offer to the Young man in the Gospel, *Go and sell that thou hast, and give to the poor, and thou shalt have treasure in Heaven*; here Christ offers heavenly treasures, for earthly treasures; unmixt treasures, for mixt treasures; perfect treasures, for imperfect treasures; satisfying treasures, for unsatisfying treasures; lasting treasures, for fading treasures; but the young man slips his opportunity, his season, and goes away sorrowful, and we never read more of him.

Mat. 21. 22, 23, 24.

Ah! Young men, young men
do

do not put off the present season, do not neglect the present day; there is no time yours, but the present time, no day yours but the present day; and therefore do not please your selves, and feed your selves with hopes of time to come, and that you will repent, but not yet; and lay hold on mercy, but not yet; and give up your selves to the Lord next week, next month, or next year; for that God that hath promised you mercy and favour, upon the day of your return, hee hath not promised to prolong your lives, till that day comes; when a Souldier was brought before *Lamacus* a Commander, for a mis-behaviour, and pleaded hee would do so no more, *Lamacus* answered (*non licet in bello bis peccare*) no man must offend twice in War; So God (especially in these Gospel daies, wherein the motions of Divine Justice are more smart and quick, than in former daies) happily will not

Often consider what the damned would give (were it in their hands) for one season of grace, for one opportunity of mercy.

suffer men twice to neglect the day of grace, and let slip the season of mercy.

Heb. 3.2.

Ah! young men, young men, you say you will bee good towards the Lord before you dye, but if you are not good towards the Lord to day, you may dye to morrow, nay, justice may leave him to bee his own executioner to morrow, who will not repent, nor seek the Lord to day. *Otho* the Emperor slew himself with his own hands, but slept so soundly the night before, that the grooms of his chamber heard him snort.

Plutarch reporteth the like of Cato.

Young men, I will suppose you to bee good accountants; now if you please to count the number, and mark the age of the Sacrifices in the Old Testament, you shall finde more Kids and Lambs offered, than Goats, and old Sheep: You have no lease of your lives, you are not sure that you shall live to *Isaacks* age, to live till your eyes wax dim; you are

Gen. 27.1

Young Men.

are not sure that you shall live to *Jacobs* years, and die, leaning upon the top of a staff. You read of them who die in their youth, and whose lives are among the unclean. Slip not the present season, neglect not this day of grace, let not Satan keep your souls and Christ any longer asunder, by telling of you, that you are too young, that hereafter will bee time enough. *Austin* tells us, that by this very temptation the Devil kept him off from receiving of Christ, from closing with Christ seven years together; hee could no sooner think of inquiring after Christ, of getting an interest in Christ, of leaving off his sinful courses, &c. but Satan would bee still a suggesting, thou art too young to leave thy drunkennesse, thou art too young to leave thy Dalilahs, to leave thy Harlots, till at last hee cryed out, how long shall I say it is too soon? why may I not repent to day? and lay hold on

Heb. 11. 21
Job 36.14

As out of the boughs of a tree are taken wedges to cleave it in peeces, so out of our own lusts, Satan works Engines to destroy us.

on Jesus Christ to day? &c. Ah young men! this is your day, this is your season, if you will not now hearken and obey, you may perish for ever. *Cesar* had a letter given him by *Artemidorus*, that morning hee went to the Senate, wherein notice was given him of all the conspiracy of his murtherers; so that with ease, hee might have prevented his death, but neglecting the reading of it, was slain, hee slipt his season, and dies for it. Ah! how many for sliping gracious seasons and opportunities, have died for ever? Soul-opportunities, are more worth than a thousand worlds; mercy is in them, grace and glory is in them, heaven and eternity is in them.

5 Motive.

Fitthly, To provoke you to bee good betimes, Consider

How just it is with God to reserve the dregs of his wrath for them, who reserve the dregs of their daies for him.

How

How can a husband imbrace that wife in her old age, who hath spent all the time of her youth, in following after strangers? Will any man receive such into his service, who hath all their daies served his enemies, & received such wounds, blows, and bruises, that renders them unfit for his service?

Ah! young men, young men, *do not thus foolishly and unwisely requite the Lord*, for all his patient waiting, his gracious wooing, and his merciful dealing with you. Ah! do not put off God to old age, for old, lame, and sick Sacrifices rarely reach as high as heaven. Is not old age very unteachable; in old age are not men very unapt to take in, and as unapt to give out? In old age (oftentimes) men are men, and no men, they have eyes, but see not, ears, but hear not, tongues, but speak not, feet, but walk not. An aged man is but a moving Anatomy, or a living mortuary; now how unlovely, how uncomely, how un-

Deut. 32.6

Multa senem circumveniunt incommoda, Horatius. Many are the inconveniences that do encompass an Old man.

unworthy, nay, how incensing, how provoking a thing must this needs bee, when men will dally with God, and put him off till their doting daies have overtaken them, till their spring is past, their Summer overpast, and they arrived at the fall of the leaf, yea, till winter colours have stained their heads with gray and hoary hairs? How provoking this is, you may see in those sad words of *Jeremiah*, Jer. 22. 21, 22. *I spake unto thee in thy prosperity, but thou saidst, I will not hear; this hath been thy manner from thy youth, that thou obeyest not my voice*: But will God put up this at their hands? no, therefore it followes in the next verse, *Surely thou shalt bee ashamed and confounded for all thy wickedness*.

Oh that young men would let this Scripture lye warm every morning upon their hearts, that so they may not dare to put off God, and provoke him to their own confusion; though you are young, and in your strength, yet

Marginal note: The reproach of the evil of wickedness is not to bee added to old age, (*Solet enim senectus esse deformis, infirma, obliviosa, edentula, lucrosa, indocilis & molesta*) saith *Plutarch*, in *Apothegm. Rom.* For old age useth to bee deformed, weak, forgetful, toothless, covetous, unteachable, unquiet.

Young Men.

yet are you ftronger than God; can you make your party good with him? if you will needs bee a provoking, provoke them that are your matches, and do not contend with him that is mightier than you, that can command you into nothing, or into Hell at pleafure.

6 Motive.

Sixthly, confider, *That the fooner you are good on earth, the greater will bee your reward in Heaven.*

The fooner you are gracious, the more at laft you will bee glorious; you read in the Scripture of a reward, of a great reward, and of a full reward; now, *thofe that are good betimes*, that know, feek, ferve and love the Lord in the fpring and morning of their youth, they are in the faireft way of gaining the greateft, and the fulleft reward.

Pfa. 58.11
Gen. 15. 1
Pfa. 19.11
Mat. 5. 12
Heb. 10. 35
John 2. 8

And this I fhall make clear by that which follows.

Firft, The fooner any man beginnes to bee really good, the more

more good hee will do in this world. Now the more good any man doth on earth, the more glory hee shall have in Heaven. Therefore my beloved Brethren, *Bee yee stedfast, unmoveable, alwaies abounding in the work of the Lord, forasmuch as you know, that your labour is not in vain in the Lord.*

Mans wages, mans reward shall bee according to his works; hee that doth most work here, shall have most reward hereafter. God will at last proportion the one to the other, the reward to the work, *Hee which soweth sparingly, shall reap sparingly, and hee which soweth bountifully, shall reap bountifully.* Though no man shall bee rewarded for his works; yet God will at last measure out happiness and blessedness to his people, according to their service, faithfulness, diligence, and work in this world. Grace is glory in the bud, and glory is grace at the full; glory is nothing else but a bright constellation of graces,

hap-

happiness, nothing but the quintessence of holinesse. Grace and glory differ (*non specie, sed gradu*) in degree, not kind, as the learned speak. Grace and glory differ very little, the one is the seed, the other is the flower, grace is glory militant, and glory is grace triumphant; and a man may as well plead for equal degrees of grace in this world, as hee may plead for equal degrees of glory in the other world. Surely the more grace here, the more glory hereafter, and the more work Christians do on earth, the more glory they shall have in Heaven; and the sooner men begin to bee good, the more good they will do in this world; and the more they do here, the more they shall have hereafter. Philosophers seems to weigh our virtues with our vices, and according to the preponderation of either, denominate us good or bad, and so deliver us up to reward or punishment.

No man can commend good Works magnificently enough, (faith *Luther*) for one work of a Christian is more precious than Heaven and Earth; and therefore all the world cannot sufficiently reward one good work. And in another place, faith the same Author, if I might have my desire, I would rather chuse the meanest work of a Country Christian (or poor maid) than all the victories and triumphs of *Alexander* the Great, and of *Julius Cæsar*.

And again, Whatsoever the Saints do, though never so small and mean, it is great and glorious, because they do all in Faith, and by the Word, faith the same Author. To prevent mistakes, you must remember, that the works that Jesus Christ will reward at last, are supernatural works; they are, 1 Works of God, 2 Wrought from God, 3 For God, 4 In God, 5 According to God, they are works that flow from supernatural Principles, and they

they are directed to supernatural ends, and performed in a supernatural way; now, the sooner a man beginnes to bee good, the more hee will abound in these good works, and the more doubtlesse any man abounds in such good works on earth, the greater reward hee shall have in Heaven; yet it must not bee forgotten, that the best actions, the best works of Hypocrites, and all men out of Christ, are but (*splendida peccata*) fair and shining sins, beautiful abominations. And as the *Phenix* in *Arabia* gathers sweet odoriferous sticks together, and then blows them with her wings, and burns her self with them; so many a carnal professor burns himself with his own good works, that is, by his expecting and trusting to receive that by his works, that is onely to be received and expected from Jesus Christ. Though all that man can do towards the meriting of Heaven, is no more than the lifting up of

David made use of his bow, but did not trust to his bow. The Dove made use of her wings, but did not trust in her wings, but in the Ark.

K

of a festraw towards the meriting of a Kingdome; yet such a proud peece man is, that hee is ready enough to say with proud *Vega*, (*Cœlum gratis non accipiam*) I will not have Heaven of free cost. A proud heart would fain have that of debt, which is meerly of grace, and desires that to bee of purchase, which God hath intended to bee of free mercy, which made one to say, that hee would swim through a Sea of Brimstone, that hee might come to Heaven at last, but hee that swims not thither, through the Sea of Christs blood, shall never come there; man must swim thither, not through brimstone, but through blood, or hee mis-carries for ever.

Merces non est debita, sed gratuita.

2 Again, the sooner a man begins to bee good, the more serviceable hee will bee to others, and the more hee will provoke others to good; now all the good that you provoke others to, by Counsel, or Carriage, shall bee put

Young Men.

put down to your account (as all the sins that men provoke others to, is put down to their accounts; *David* did but send a Letter concerning the death of *Uriah*, and the charge cometh, *Thou hast slain Uriah with the Sword*) the more I stir up others to sow, the more at last I shall reap; the sooner a man beginnes to bee good, the more good hee will do, the more serviceable hee will bee in the Town or City where hee dwells, in the Family where hee lives, among his Relations (Wife, Children, Kindred, Servants, &c.) with whom he converses.

The sooner a man beginnes to bee gracious, the sooner and the more useful will his arts, his parts, his gifts, his graces, his mercies, his experiences, his life, his labours, his prayers, his counsels, his examples, bee, to all that are with him, to all that are about him.

Lilmod Lelammed, wee therefore learn

2 Sam. 12. 8, 9
Isa. 38. 3
Neh. 13. 14

Synesius speaks of some, who having a treasure of rare abilities in them, would as soon part with their hearts, as their conceptions; but such are rather monsters than men.

learn that wee may teach, is a Proverb among the *Rabbins*. And I do therefore lay in, and lay up (saith the Heathen) that I may draw forth again, and lay out for the good of many.

Ah! Young men! Young men, as you would be useful and serviceable to many, beginne to bee good betimes, and to lay in and lay up, and lay out betimes, for the profit and advantage of others. *Augustine* accounted nothing his own, that hee did not communicate to others. The Bee doth store her Hive out of all sorts of Flowers, for the common benefit. 'Tis a base and unworthy spirit, for a man to make himself the centre of all his actions. The very Heathen man could say, that a mans Countrey, and his friends, and others challenge a great part of him: And indeed the best way to do our selves good, is to bee a doing good to others; the best way to gather, is to scatter; Memorable

Young Men. 133

morable is that story of *Pyrhias* a Merchant of *Ithaca*, who at Sea espying an aged man, a Captive in a Pyrates Ship, took compassion of him, and redeemed him, and bought his Commodities which the Pyrate had taken from him, which were certain barrels of Pitch; The old man perceiving, that not for any good service hee could do him, nor for the gain of that commodity, but meerly out of charity and pitty hee had done this, discovered a great masse of treasure hidden in the pitch, whereby the Merchant in a very short time became very rich, at which very time God made that Word good; *Hee that soweth liberally, shall reap liberally*; and that word, *The liberal soul shall bee made fat*; and that word, *The liberal deviseth liberal things, and by liberal things shall hee stand.* It is fabled of *Midas*, that what ever hee touched, hee turned it into gold: It is certain, that a liberal hand, a liberal

2 Cor. 9.6

P10.11.25

Isa. 32.8.

K 3

ral heart turns all into gold, into gain, as Scripture and Experience do abundantly evidence: now if you put all these things together, nothing is more evident, than that those that begin to bee good betimes, are in the ready way, the high way to bee high in Heaven, when they shall cease from breathing on earth; and therefore young men, as you would be high in Heaven, as you would have a great reward, a full reward, a massie weighty Crown, O labour to be good betimes! labour to get acquaintance with the Lord, and an interest in the Lord, in the spring and morning of your daies.

7 Motive.

The seventh Motive or consideration to provoke and incite you to bee good betimes, is, *To consider that the Lord is very much affected, and taken with your seeking of him, and following after him in the spring and morning of your youth.*

Go and cry in the ears of *Jerusalem.*

salem, saying, *I remember thee, the kindness of thy youth, the love of thine espousals, when thou wentest after me in the wilderness, in a land that was not sown.* Jer. 2. 2.

Ah! how kindly, how sweetly did the Lord take this at their hands, that they followed him in their youth, while their bones were full of marrow, while they were strong and fit for service, while nature was fresh, lively and vigorous; In the Law, God called for the first of all things, hee required not onely the first fruits, but the very first of the first; The first of the first-fruits of thy land, *Thou shalt bring into the house of the Lord thy God.* God is the first being, the first good, and therefore deserves the first of the first, and the best of the best; the first and the best is not too good for him, who is goodness it self. God in that of *Leviticus* 2. 14. is so passionately set upon having the first of the first, that hee will not stay till the green Exod. 23. 19.

Tis truly said of God, that hee is *Omnia super omnia*.

green ears of Corn bee ripe, but will have the green ears of Corn dried in the fire, left hee should lose his longing.

As many young women, and sickly children cannot stay till the fruit be ripe, but must have it while it is green; even so saith God, my heart, my desires, are so vehemently set upon the first fruits, the first things, that I cannot stay, I cannot satisfie my self without them; and what would God teach us by all this, but to serve him with the first-fruits of our age, the prim-rose of our childhood, the morning of your youth. God hath given you of the best, do not put him off with the worst, with the worst of your time, the worst of your daies, the worst of your strength, lest hee swear in his wrath, that you shall never enter into his rest.

8 Motive.
The eighth Motive or Consideration to provoke you to bee good

Young Men.   137

good betimes, to seek and serve the Lord in the morning of your youth, is, to consider, that *This may bee a special means to prevent many black temptations, and an incouragement to withstand all temptations, that you may meet with from a tempting Devil, and a tempting world.*

An early turning to the Lord will prevent many temptations to despair, many temptations to neglect the means openly, to despise the means secretly: many temptations about the being of God, the goodness, faithfulness, truth and justice of God; temptations to despair, temptations to lay violent hands on a mans self; temptations to question all that God hath said, and that Christ hath suffered, arises many times from mens delaying, and putting off of God to the last; all which, with many others, are prevented by a mans seeking and serving of the Lord in the spring and morning of his youth. It is reported of the Harts of *Scythia*

Early Converts will never have cause to say, as that despairing Pope said, the Cross could do him no good, because hee had so often sold it away.

thin, that they teach their young ones to leap from Bank to Bank, from Rock to Rock, from one Turf to another (by leaping before them) by which means when they are hunted, no beast of prey can ever take them; so when persons exercise themselves in godliness, when they are young, when they leap from one measure of holiness to another, when they are in the morning of their daies; Satan that mighty hunter after souls, may pursue them with his temptations, but hee shall not overtake them, hee shall not prevail over them. As you see in *Moses*, *Joseph*, *Daniel*, and the three Children, these knew the Lord, and gave up themselves to the Lord in the prime and Prim-rose of their Youth; and these were all temptation-proof; Satan and the World pursued them, but could not overtake them; when the Devil and the World had done their worst, the young mens bows abode

Heb. 11.
Gen. 39.
Dan. 3. ult.

bode in strength, and their hands (to resist) were made strong by the hands of the mighty God of *Jacob*. *Ego non sum ego*, said that young convert, when tempted, I am not the man that I was.

Luther tells of a young Virgin that used to resist all temptations, with this, *Christianus sum*, I am a Christian. Early Converts may say, when tempted, as hee, tell mee not Satan what I have been, but what I am, and will bee; or as hee in the like case, whatsoever I was, I am now in Christ, a new creature, and that is it which troubleth thee; or, as hee, the more desperate my disease was, the more I admire the Physician. Yea, thou mayest yet strain it a peg higher, and say, the greater my sins were, the greater is my honour. As the Devils which once *Mary Magdalen* had, are mentioned for her glory. When *Pyrrhus* tempted *Fabritius* the first day with an Elephant, so huge and monstrous

Gen. 49. 23, 24.

Bernard. Beza. Augustin. Such as thou art now, I was once, but such as I am now, thou wilt never be, said *Diogenes* to a base fellow that told him, hee had once been a forger of mony.

strous a beast, as before he had not seen, the next day with mony, and promises of honour; hee answered, I fear not thy force, I am too wise, for thy fraud.

Ah! young men, young men, as you would bee free from the saddest and darkest temptations; and as you would bee armed against all temptations; O labour as for life, to bee good betimes! seek and serve the Lord in the morning of your youth; no way like this for the preventing earth-quakes, heart-quakes, stormy daies, and winter nights, &c.

9 Motive.

The ninth Motive or Consideration to stir up young men to bee good betimes, to seek and serve the Lord in the spring and morning of their youth, is, *To consider the worth and excellency of souls.*

A soul is a spiritual immortal substance, it is capable of the knowledge of God, it is capable of union with God, of communion

Luk. 23. 13
Matth. 19. 28
Act. 7. ult.

nion with God, and of a bles- | Phil. 1.23
sed and happy fruition of
God.

Christ left his Fathers bosome
for the good of souls; hee assum-
ed mans nature for the salvati-
on of mans soul; Christ pray- | Heb. 2.13,
ed for souls, hee sweat for souls, | 14,15, 16
hee wept for souls, hee bled for
souls, hee hung on the Cross for
souls, hee trode the Wine-press | Isa. 63.3,4
of his Fathers wrath for souls, hee
died for souls, hee rose again from
death for souls, hee ascended for | Joh. 14. 1,
souls, hee intercedes for souls, and | 2, 3.
all the glorious preparations that
hee hath been a making in Heaven
these sixteen hundred years, is for
souls.

Ah! young men, young men, do not play the Courtier with your precious souls, the Courtier doth all things late, hee rises late, dines late, sups late, goes to bed late, repents late.

Ah! Sirs, the good of your souls is before all, and above all other things in the world, to bee
first

first regarded and provided for, and that partly, becauſe it is the beſt and more noble part of man, and partly, becauſe therein moſtly and properly is the Image of God ſtampt, and partly, becauſe it is the firſt converted, and partly, becauſe it ſhall bee the firſt and moſt glorified.

Ah! Young men, young men, if they bee worſe than Infidels, that make no proviſion for their Families; what monſters are they that make not proviſion for their own ſouls? this will bee bitterneſs in the end.

Cæſar Borgias being ſick to death, lamentingly ſaid, When I lived I provided for every thing but Death; now I muſt dye, and am unprovided to dye; this was a dart at his heart, and it will at laſt bee a dagger at yours, who feaſt your bodies, but ſtarve your ſouls; who make liberal proviſion for your ignoble part, but no proviſion for your more noble part.

O anima Dei inſignita imagine, deſponſata fide, donata ſpiritu. Bern.

1 Tim. 5. 8

If they deserve a hanging, who feast their slaves, and starve their Wives, that make provision for their enemies, but none for their friends; how will you escape hanging in Hell, who make provision for every thing, yea, for your very lusts, but make no provision for your immortal souls? Wee hate the *Turks* for selling Christians for slaves, and what shall wee think then of those who sell themselves, their precious souls, for toies and trifles that cannot profit? who practically say, what once a prophane Noble man of *Naples* verbally said, *viz.* that hee had two souls in his body, one for God, and another for whosoever would buy it.

Ah! young men, young men, do not pawn your souls, do not sell your souls, do not exchange away your souls, do not trifle and fool away your precious souls, they are Jewels, more worth than a thousand worlds, yea, than Heaven and Earth; if they are safe, all

Jam. 3. Hos. 7. 13, 14

Callenuceus relates this story.

all is safe; but if they are lost, all is lost, God lost, and Christ lost, and the society of glorious Angels and blessed Saints lost, and Heaven lost, and that for ever. *Granctensis* tells of a woman that was so affected with souls miscarryings, that shee besought God to stop up the passage into Hell with her soul and body, that none might have entrance.

Ah! that all young persons were so affected with the worth and excellency of their souls, and so allarmed with the hazard and danger of losing their souls, as that they may in the spring and morning of their daies enquire after the Lord, and seek him, and serve him with all their might, that so their precious and immortal souls may bee safe and happy for ever; but if all this will not do, then in the last place,

10 Motive.

Tenthly, Consider, Young men, *That God will at last bring you to a reckoning*; Hee will at last

Young Men.

last bring you to judgement. *Rejoyce, O young man, in thy youth, and let thy heart chear thee in the daies of thy youth, and walk in the waies of thine heart, and in the sight of thine eies; but know thou, that for all these things, God will bring thee unto judgement.* In these words you have two things, 1 An ironical concession, hee bids him rejoyce, &c. hee yeelds him what hee would have, by an irony, by way of mockage and bitter scoff. Now thou art young, and strong, lively, and lusty, and thy bones are full of marrow; thou art resolved to bee proud, and scornfull, to indulge the flesh, and to follow thy delights, and pleasure; well take thy course if thou darest, or if thou hast a minde to it, if thy heart bee so set upon it. *Rejoyce in thy youth, &c.* The second is a commination, or a sad and severe præmonition. *But know thou, that for all these things, God will bring thee into judgement; will bring thee,*

Eccl. 11. 9.

Hierom stil thought that that noise was in his ears (*surgite mortui, & venite ad judicium*) arise you dead, and come to judgement

these

these words import two things, first, the unwillingness of youth to come to judgement; secondly, the unavoidablenesse that youth must come to judgement; but how soon you shall bee brought to judgement, is onely known to God.

Augustine confesses in one of his books, that as long as his conscience was gnawed with the guilt of some youthful lust, hee was once insnared with, the very hearing of a day of judgement, was even a Hell to him.

Histories tell us of a young man, who being for some Capital offence condemned to dye, grew gray in one nights space, and was therefore pittied, and spared.

Ah! Young men, young men, that the serious thoughts of this great day, may put you upon breaking off the sins of your youth; and the dedicating of your selves to the knowledge, love, and service of the Lord, in the

the spring and flower of your daies. Ah young men, consider the errours of your lives; the wickednesse of your hearts, the sinfulnesse of your wayes, and that strickt account that ere long you must bee brought to before the Judge of all the world.

The Heathens themselves had some kinde of dread and expectation of such a day; and therefore when *Paul* spake of Judgement to come, *Fœlix* trembled, though a Heathen.

The bringing into judgement is a thing which is known by reason, and is clear by the light of Nature; wherefore in *Austria* one of the Nobles dying, who had lived fourscore and thirteen years, and had spent all his life in pleasures and delights, never being troubled with any infirmity, and this being told to *Frederick* the Emperour, from hence saith hee, wee may conclude, the souls immortality; for if there bee a God

Act.24.25

The Philosophers had some dreams of a severe day of accounts; as appeareth by *Plato's Georgl*, & many passages in *Tulli*, &c.

that ruleth this world (as Divines and Philosophers do teach, and that hee is just, no one denieth; surely there are other places to which souls after death do go, and do receive for their deeds, either reward, or punishment, for here wee see, that neither rewards are given to the good, nor punishments to the evil.

Ah! Young men, knowing therefore the terrour of the Lord, and the terrour of this day, Oh! that you would bee perswaded to flee from the wrath to come; to cast away the Idols of your souls, to repent and bee converted in the prime-rose of your youth, that your sins may bee blotted out when the times of refreshing shall come from the presence of the Lord, or else woe, woe to you that ever you were Born. I have read a story of one, who being risen from the dead, and being asked in what condition hee was, hee made answer, no man doth beleeve, no man doth beleeve,

Eneas Sylvius.

2 Cor. 5. 9, 10, 11

Act. 3. 19

beleeve, no man doth beleeve. And being further asked what he meant by that repetition, hee answered, no man doth beleeve, how exactly God examineth, how strictly God judgeth, how severely hee punisheth. Oh that the waies of most young persons did not declare to all the world that they do not, and that they will not beleeve the dread, and terrour of that day, that will admit of no plea, nor place for Apology or appeal; the highest and last Tribunal, can never bee appealed from, or repealed.

Now if for all that hath been said, you are resolved to spend the flower of your daies, and the prime of your strength, in the service of sin and the world, then know, that no tongue can expresse, no heart can conceive that trouble of minde, that terrour of soul, that horror of conscience, that fear and amazement, that weeping and wailing, that crying and roaring, that sighing and groaning,

The Turks have a tradition, and frantick opinion, that wicked men shall at the great day carry their sinnes in latchets after their Captain Cain, but well would it bee for them, if this should be all their punishment in that great day.

that cursing and banning, that stamping and tearing, that wringing of hands, and gnashing of teeth, that shall certainly attend you, when God shall bring you into judgement for all your loosnesse, and lightnesse, for all your wickednesse, and wantonnesse, for all your prophanenesse, and basenesse, for all your neglect of God, your grieving the comforter, your trampling under foot the blood of a Saviour, for your despising of the means, for your prizing earth above heaven, and the pleasures of this World above the pleasures that bee at Gods right hand.

Oh! how will you wish in that day when your sins shall be charged on you, when justice shall bee armed against you, when conscience shall bee gnawing within you, when the World shall bee a Flaming fire about you, when the gates of heaven shall be shut against you, and the flame of Hell ready to take hold of you, when

Chrysostom speaking of this day, saith for Christ at this day to say, depart from me, is a thing more terrible than a thousand hells, Chry. Hom. ad Pop. Antioch.

Angels and Saints shall sit in judgement upon you, and for ever turn their faces from you, when evil spirits shall bee terrifying of you, and Jesus Christ for ever disowning of you, how will you (I say) wish in that day that you had never been born, or that you might now bee unborn, or that your mothers wombs had proved your Tombs? O how will you then wish to bee turned into a bird, a beast, a stock, a stone, a Toad, a Tree! O that our immortal souls were mortal, O that wee were nothing, O that wee were any thing but what wee are.

    I have read a remarkable story of a King, that was heavy and sad, and wept, which when his Brother saw, hee asked him why hee was so pensive? because (saith he) I have judged others, and now I must bee judged my self: And why (saith his brother) do you so take on for this, it will (happily) bee a long time ere

Joan Damasc. et Author. Anonym. de quat. Noviss. Impress. Daven. Ann. 1494

ere that day come, and besides that, it is but a slight matter. The King said little to it for the present.

Now it was a custome in that Countrey, when any had committed Treason, there was a Trumpet sounded at his door in the night time, and hee was next day brought out to bee executed, now the King commanded a Trumpet to be sounded at his brothers door in the night time, who awakening out of his sleep, when hee heard i, arose, and came quaking and trembling to the King; How now saith the King? what's the matter you are so affrighted? I am saith hee attatched of Treason, and next morning I shall bee executed; why saith the King to him again, are you so troubled at that, knowing that you shall bee judged by your Brother, and for a matter that your Conscience tells you, you are clear of? How much more therefore may I bee afraid, seeing that

that God shall judge mee, and not in a matter that my Conscience frees mee of, but of that whereof I am guilty? and beside this, if the worst come, it is but a temporary death you shall dye, but I am liable to death eternal both of body and soul. I will leave the Application to those young persons, that put this day afar off, and whom no arguments will move to be good betimes, and to acquaint themselves with the Lord in the morning of their youth.

But now to those young men and women who beginne to seek, serve, and love the Lord in the prime-rose of their daies, the day of judgement will bee to them (*melodia in aura, jubilum in corde*) like musick in the ear, and a jubilee in the heart, this day will be to them, a day of refreshing, a day of redemption, a day of vindication, a day of Coronation, a day of Consolation, a day of Salvation, it will bee to them a Marriage day, a Harvest day,

Act. 3. 19, 20, 21, 22.
Mic. 7. 7, 8, 9, 10, 11.
Rev. 19. 6, 7, 8, 9, 10.
Mat. 25. 34. to v. 41

a pay day: Now the Lord will pay them for all the prayers they have made, for all the Sermons they have heard, for all the tears they have shed; in this great day Christ will remember all the individual Offices of Love and Friendship shewed to any of his, now he will mention many things for their honour and comfort that they never minded, now the least and lowest acts of love and pitty towards his, shall bee interpreted as a special kindnesse shewed to himself. Now the Crown shall bee set upon their heads, and the Royal Robe put upon their backs, now all the World shall see that they have not served the Lord for naught: Now Christ will pass over all their weaknesses, and make honourable mention of all the services they have performed, of all the mercies they have improved, and of all the great things that for his name and glory, they have suffered.

2 Tim. 4. 8
Mal. 3. 17. 18.

CHAP.

CHAP. V.

Quest. BUt here an apt question may bee moved, *viz.* whether at this great day, the sins of the Saints shall bee brought into the judgement of discussion and discovery or no, whether the Lord will in this day publikely manifest; proclaim, and make mention of the sins of his people, or no?

I humbly judge according to my present light, that hee will not; and my reasons for it are these, *viz.*

The first is drawn from Christs judicial proceedings in the last day, set down largely and clearly in the 25. of *Matthew*, where hee innumerateth onely the good works they had done, but takes no notice of the spots and blots, of the stains and blemishes, of the infirmities, and innormities, of the weaknesses and wickednesses of his people. My

Second Reason is taken from Christs vehement protestations that

Deut. 32. 4, 5, 6

that they shall not come into judgement, Joh. 5.24. *Verily, Verily, I say unto you, he that heareth my word, and beleeveth on him that sent me, hath everlasting life, and shall not come into condemnation, but is passed from death unto life.* Those words, shall not come into condemnation, are not rightly translated, the Original is, ἐις κρίσιν, shall not come into judgement, not into damnation, as you read it in all your English Books, I will not say what should put men upon this exposition, rather than a true translation of the Original word: further, it is very observable, that no Evangelist useth this double asseveration, but *John*, and he never useth it but in matters of greatest weight and importance, and to shew the earnestnesse of his spirit, and to stir us up to better attention, and to put the thing asserted out of all question, and beyond all contradiction; as when we would put a thing for ever out of all question, we do it

Vide Aquin. 87. Suppl. Est. in l. 4. Sen. dist. 47.

Joh.1.51. ch.3.3.11. ch.6.26. 32.47.53. &c.

it by a double asseveration, verily, verily, 'tis so, &c.

Thirdly, because his not bringing their sinnes into judgement, doth most and best agree with many precious and glorious expressions that wee finde scattered (as so many shining sparkling Pearls) up and down in Scripture, as First, With those of Gods blotting out the sinnes of his People. *I, even I am hee that blotteth out thy transgressions for my own sake, and will not remember thy sins.* Isa. 43. 25. *I have blotted out as a thick cloud thy transgressions, and as a cloud thy sinnes.* Isa. 44. 22. Who is this that blots out transgressions? hee that hath the keies of heaven and Hell, at his girdle, that opens and no man shuts, that shuts and no man opens, hee that hath the Power of life and death, of condemning and absolving, of killing and making alive, hee it is that blots out transgressions; if an under Officer should blot out an inditement, that perhaps might

might do a man no good, a man might for all that bee at last cast by the Judge; but when the Judge or King shall blot out the inditement with their own hand, then the inditement cannot return; now this is every Beleevers case and happiness.

Secondly, To those glorious expressions, of Gods not remembring of their sinnes any more, Isa. 43. 25. *And I will not remember thy sinnes; And they shall teach no more every man his neighbour, and every man his brother, saying, know the Lord, for they shall all know mee from the least of them, to the greatest of them, saith the Lord, for I will forgive their iniquity, and I will remember their sinne no more.* So the Apostle, *for I will bee merciful to their unrighteousnesse, and their sinnes, and their iniquities will I remember no more.*

And again the same Apostle saith, *This is the Covenant that I will make with them after those days;*

Jer. 31. 34

Heb. 8. 12

daies, saith the Lord, *I will put my Laws into their hearts, and in their minds will I write them: and their sins and iniquities will I remember no more.*

The meaning is, their iniquities shall quite bee forgotten, I will never mention them more, I will never take notice of them more, they shall never hear more of them from mee, though God hath an iron memory to remember the sinnes of the wicked; yet hee hath no memory to remember the sinnes of the Righteous.

Thirdly, His not bringing their Sinnes into judgement, doth most and best agree with those blessed expressions, of his casting their Sinnes into the depth of the Sea; and of his casting them behind his back. *Hee will turn again, he will have compassion upon us, hee will subdue our Iniquities, and thou wilt cast all their sinnes into the depths of the Sea,* where sinne is once pardoned, the remission stands

---

Heb. 10. 17 That which *Cicero* said flatteringly of *Cæsar*, is truly affirmed of God, *Nihil oblivisci solet præter injurias*, hee forgetteth nothing but the wrongs that daily are done him by his.

Mic. 7. 19

stands never to bee repealed, pardoned sinnes shall never come in account against the pardoned man, before God any more, for so much doth this borrowed speech import: if a thing were cast into a River, it might bee brought up again, or if it were cast upon the Sea, it might bee discerned, and taken up again, but when it is cast into the depths, the bottome of the Sea, it can never bee boyed up again.

By the Metaphor in the Text, the Lord would have us to know, the sinnes pardoned shall rise no more, they shal never be seen more, they shall never come on the account more; hee will so drown their sinnes, that they shall never come up before him the second time.

And so much that other scripture imports. *Behold, for Peace I had great Bitternesse, but thou hast in love to my soul delivered it from the pit of Corruption:*

Isa. 38. 17.

ruption; *for thou hast cast all my sins behind thy back*; these last words are a borrowed speech, taken from the manner of men, who are wont to cast behinde their backs, such things as they have no minde to see, regard, or remember. A gracious soul hath alwaies his sins before his face (*I acknowledge my transgressions, and my sin is ever before mee*;) and therefore no wonder if the Lord cast them behinde his back. The Father soon forgets, and casts behinde his back those faults that the childe remembers, and hath alwaies in his eyes; so doth the Father of spirits.

Psa. 51. 3.

Fourthly, *His not bringing their sinnes into judgement*, doth best agree with that sweet and choice expression of Gods pardoning the sins of his people; *And I will cleanse them from all their iniquity, whereby they have sinned against mee; and I will pardon all their iniquities, whereby they have sinned, and whereby they have transgressed against mee*. So Micha

Jer. 33. 8.

M   who

*Mic.*7.18.   *who is a God like unto thee, that pardoneth iniquity, and passes by the transgressions of the remnant of his heritage* (as though hee would not see it, but wink at it) *hee retaineth not his anger for ever, because he delighteth in Mercy.* The Hebrew word (*Nose* from *Nasa*) that is here rendred, pardoneth, signifies a taking away; when God pardons sin, hee takes it sheer away, that if it should bee sought for, yet it could not bee found, as the Prophet speaks; *In those days, and in that time saith the Lord, the iniquity of Israel shall be sought for,*
Jer. 50.20 *and there shall bee none; and the sins of Judah, and they shall not bee found, for I will pardon them whom I reserve*; and those words, *and passeth by,* in the (aforecited) seventh of *Micha,* and the 18. according to the Hebrew (*Vegnober Gnal*)

עָבַר

Gnabar, he passed over.

is, *and passeth over, God passeth over the transgression of his heritage;* that is, hee takes no notice of it; as a man in a deep muse, or as one that hath haste of businefs, seeth

not

not things before him, his mind being busied about other matters, hee neglects all to mind his businesse. As *David* when hee saw in *Mephibosheth* the feature of his friend *Jonathan*, took no notice of his lamenesse, or any other defect, or deformity: So God beholding in his people the glorious image of his Son, winks at all their faults and deformities, which made *Luther* say, *do with mee what thou wilt, since thou hast pardoned my sin*; and what is it to pardon sin, but not to mention sin? Isa. 40. 1,2.

Fifthly, *In his not bringing their sinnes into the judgement of Discussion and Discovery*, Doth best agree to those expressions of Forgiving, and covering; *Blessed is hee whose transgression is forgiven, whose sinne is covered*. In the Original it is in the plural, Blessednesses, loe, here is a plurality of blessings, a chain of pearls. Psal. 32. 1.

The like expression you have in the 85. *Psalm*, and the 2 verse.

Thou

Thou hast forgiven the iniquity of thy people, thou hast covered all their sin. Selah. For the understanding of these Scriptures aright, take notice, that to cover, is a Metaphorical expression, covering is such an action, which is opposed to disclosure; to bee covered, is to bee so hid and closed, as not to appear. Some make the Metaphor from filthy loathsome objects, which are covered from our eyes, as dead carkasses are buried under the ground; some from Garments, that are put upon us to cover our nakedness; others from the Egyptians that were drowned in the red Sea, and so covered with water; others from a great gulf in the earth, that is filled up and covered with earth, injected into it; and others make it in the last place an allusive expression to the mercy-seat, over which was a covering: Now all these Metaphors in the general, tend to shew this, that the Lord will not look, hee will not see,

Sic velantur, ut in judicio non revelentur.

see, hee will not take notice of the sins hee hath pardoned, to call them any more to a judicial account.

As when a Prince reads over many treasons, and rebellions, and meets with such and such which hee hath pardoned, hee reads on, hee passeth by, hee takes no notice of them, the pardoned person shall never hear more of them, hee will never call him to account for those sinnes more. So here, &c. When *Cæsar* was painted, hee put his finger upon his scar, his wart. God puts his fingers upon all his peoples scars and warts, upon all their weaknesses and infirmities, that nothing can bee seen but what is fair and lovely; *Thou art all fair, my love, and there is no spot in thee*, Cant. 4. 7.

Sixthly, It best agrees to that expression of not imputing of sin. *Blessed is the man to whom the Lord imputeth not iniquity, and in whose spirit there is no guile.* So the Apostle in that, *Rom.* 4. 6, 7, 8. now

Psal. 32. 2

not

not to impute iniquity, is not to charge iniquity, not to set iniquity upon his score, who is blessed and pardoned, &c.

Seventhly and lastly, it best agrees with that expression that you have in the 103. *Psalm* and the 11, and 12 *verses. For as the Heaven is high above the Earth, so great is his mercy towards them that fear him: As far as the East is from the West, so far hath he removed our transgressions from us.* What a vast distance is there betwixt the East and the West? of all visible latitudes, this is the greatest; and thus much for the third Argument. The

Fourth Argument, that prevails with me, to judge that Jesus Christ will not bring the sins of the saints into the judgement of discussion, and discovery in the great day, is because it seems unsuitable to three considerable things, for Jesus Christ to proclaim the infirmities and miscarriages of his people to all the world.

First

First, it seems to bee unsuitable to the glory and solemnity of that day, which to the Saints will be a day of refreshing, a day of restitution, a day of redemption, a day of coronation, as hath been already proved; now how suitable to this great day of solemnity, the proclamation of the Saints sins will be, I leave the Reader to judge.

Secondly, It seems unsuitable to all those near and dear relations, that Jesus Christ stands in towards his, hee stands in the relation of a *Father, a Brother, a Head, a Husband, a Friend, an Advocate*; Now are not all these by the Law of relations, bound rather to hide and keep secret (at least from the world) the weaknesses and infirmities of their near and dear relations, and is not Christ? is not Christ much more? By how much hee is more a *Father, a Brother, a Head, a Husband, &c.* in a spiritual way, than any others can bee in a natural way, &c.

Isa. 9. 6
Heb. 2. 11, 12
Ephes. 1. 21, 22
Rev. 19. 7
John 15. 1
Joh. 2. 1, 2

Third-

Thirdly, It seems very unsuitable to what the Lord Jesus requires of his in this world, the Lord requires that his people should cast a mantle of love, of wisdome, of silence, and secresie over one anothers weaknesses and infirmities.

Pro. 10.12
1 Pet. 4.8.

Hatred stirreth up strifes, but love covereth all sins; loves mantle is very large; love will finde a hand, a plaister to clap upon every sore. *Flavius Vespasianus* (the Emperor) was very ready to conceal his friends vices, and as ready to reveal their virtues: So is divine love in the hearts of the Saints;

Mat. 18. 15

If thy Brother offend thee, go and tell him his fault between him and thee alone; if hee shall hear thee, thou hast gained thy Brother. As the Pills of reprehension are to bee gilded, and sugred over with much gentleness, and softness; so they are to bee given in secret, tell him between him and thee alone. Tale-bearers, and Tale-hearers are alike abominable,
Heaven

Young Men.

Heaven is too hot, and too holy a place for them, *Psal.* 15. 3. Now will Jesus Christ have us carry it thus towards offending Christians, and will hee himself act otherwise? nay, is it an evil in us to lay open the weaknesses and infirmities of the Saints to the World? and will it bee an excellency, a glory, a virtue in Christ, to do it in the great day? &c.

A fifth Argument is this, It is the glory of a man to pass over a transgression. *The discretion of a man deferreth his anger, and it is his glory to passe over a transgression*, or to pass by it, as wee do by persons or things, wee know not, or would take no notice of. Now *is it the glory of a man to passe over a transgression*, and will it not much more bee thee glory of Christ, silently to pass over the transgressions of his people, in that great day? The greater the treasons and rebellions are that a Prince passes over, and takes no notice of, the more is it his ho-

Prov. 19. 11.

Non amo quemquam nisi offendam, said a Heathen.

honour, and glory; and so doubtlesse it will be Christs in that great day, to passe over all the treasons and rebellions of his people, to take no notice of them, to forget them, as well as to forgive them.

The Heathens have long since observed, that in nothing man came nearer to the glory and perfection of God himselfe, than in goodnesse and clemency. Surely if it be such an honor to man, *to pass over a transgression*, it cannot bee a dishonour to Christ, to pass over the transgressions of his people, hee having already buried them in the Sea of his blood. Again faith *Solomon*, *It is the glory of God to conceal a thing.* And why it should not make for the glory of divine love to conceal the sins of the Saints in that great day, I know not: and whether the concealing the sinnes of the Saints in that great day, will not make most for their joy, and wicked mens sorrow, for their comfort, and wicked mens terrour and torment, I will leave you to

Prov. 25,7

to judge, and time and experience to decide; And thus much for the resolution of that great question. Having done with the Motives that may incourage and provoke young men to bee good betimes, to know, love, seek, and serve the Lord, in the spring and morning of their days,

CHAP. VI.

I Shall now come to those directions and helps, that must (by assistance from Heaven) bee put in practice, if ever you would be good betimes, and serve the Lord in the prim-rose of your dayes. Now all that I shall say, will fall under these two heads.

First, *Some things you must carefully, and warily decline, and arm your selves against,* and

Secondly, *There are other things that you must prosecute and follow.*

First, *There are some things that you must warily decline*, and they are these.

1 Di-

1 Direction.

First, *If ever you would bee good betimes, if you would be gracious in the Spring and morning of your youth, Oh! then take heed of putting the day of death far from you.*

Amos 6. 3

Young men are very prone to look upon death afar off, to put it at a great distance from them; they are apt to say to death, as *Pharaoh* said to *Moses*, *Get thee from mee, and let mee see thy face no more*; if old men discourse to them of death, they are ready to answer, as the High-Priest did *Judas* (in a different case) *what is that to us? look you unto it*: we know sickness will come, and death is a debt that wee must all pay, but surely these guests are a great way from us, for doth not *David* say, *the daies of a man are threescore years and ten?* wee have calculated our nativities, and we cannot abate a day, a minute, a moment, of *threescore and ten*; and therefore it is even a death to us to think of death, there being so great a distance between our birth-day

Exod. 10. 28

Mat. 27.4

Psa. 90.10

day, and our dying-day, as wee have cast up the account.

Ah young men! it is sad, it is very sad, when you are so wittily wicked, as to say with those in *Ezekiel*, *Behold they of the house of Israel say, the vision that hee seeth is for many daies to come, and hee prophesieth of the times that are afar off.* Ezek. 12. 27.

Ah! Young men, young men, by putting far away this day, you gratifie Satan, you strengthen sin, you provoke the Lord, you make the work of faith and repentance more hard and difficult; you lay a sad foundation for the greatest fears and doubts.

Ah! How soon may that sad word bee fulfilled upon you. *The Lord of that servant, that saith his Lord delayeth his coming, shall come in a day when hee looketh not for him, and in an hour that hee is not aware of, and shall cut him asunder (or cut him off) and appoint him his portion with Hypocrites, there shall bee weeping and gnashing of teeth.* Mat. 24. 48, 49, 50, 51 *teeth.* When *Sodom*, when *Pharaoh*, when *Agag*, when *Amaleck*, when *Haman*, when *Herod*, when *Nebuchadnezzar*, when *Belshazzar*, when *Dives*, when the fool in the Gospel, were all in their prime, their pride, when they were all in a flourishing state, and upon the very top of their glory, how strangely, how suddenly, how sadly, how fearfully, how wonderfully, were they brought down to the grave, to hell!

Ah young man! who art thou, and what is thy name or fame, what is thy power or place, what is thy dignity or glory, that thou darest promise thy self an exemption from sharing in as sad a portion as ever Justice gave to those who were once very high, who were seated among the stars, but are now brought down to the sides of the pit? I have read a story of one, that gave a young Prodigal a Ring with a Deaths head, on this condition, that hee should one hour daily for seven days

Isa. 13. 10, 11, 12, 13, 14, 15, 16, 17

Young Men.

days together, look and think upon it, which bred a great change in his life.

Ah young men! the serious thoughts of death may do that for you, that neither friends, counsel, examples, prayers, sermons, tears have not done to this very day. Well, remember this, to labour not to dye, is labour in vain, and to put this day far from you, and to live without fear of death, is to dye living. Death seizeth on old men, and lays wait for the youngest. Death is oftentimes as near to the young mans back, as it is to the old mans face.

Senibus mors in januis, adolescentibus in insidiis, Bernard. De convers. ad Cler. c. 14.

It is storied of *Charles* the fourth King of *France*, that being one time affected with the sense of his many and great sins, he fetcht a deep sigh, and said to his wife, By the help of God, I will now so carry my self all my life long, that I will never offend him more; which words he had no sooner uttered, but he fell down dead and dyed.

Do not young men put this day far from you, lest you are suddenly surprized, and then you cry out, (when too late) *a Kingdome for a Christ, a Kingdome for a Christ*; as once Crookt-back Richard the Third in his Distresse, *a Kingdome for a horse, a Kingdome for a horse.*

Ah young men! did you never hear of a young man that cryed out; *Oh! I am so sick, that I cannot live, and yet (woful wretch that I am) so sinful, that I dare not dye; Oh that I might live! Oh that I might dye! Oh that I might do neither!* Well young men, remember this, the frequent, the serious thoughts of death will prevent many a sin, it will arm you against many temptations, it will secure you from many afflictions, it will keep you from doting on the world, it will make you do much in a little time, it will make Death easie when it comes, and it will make you look out betimes for a Kingdome that

2 Pet. 1. 13,14
Eccl. 9. 10

shakes not, for riches that corrupt not, and for glory that fadeth not away. Therefore do not, O do not put the day of death far from you. Take heed of crying *Cras, Cras,* to morrow, to morrow, saith *Luther,* for a man lives forty years before hee knows himself to bee a fool, and by that time hee sees his folly, his life is finished, so men dye before they begin to live.

2 Direction

Secondly, *If you would bee good betimes, then take heed of leaning to your own understanding.*

This Counsel wise *Solomon* gives to his son (or the young men in his time) *My Son, forget not my Law, but let thy heart keep my Commandements: Trust in the Lord with all thy heart, and lean not to thy own understanding.*

Youth is the age of folly, of vain-hopes, and over-grown confidence. Ah! how wise might many

Pro. 3.1.5 Lean not, is a Metaphor from an old or sick man leaning on his staff, &c.

many have been, had they not been too early wise in their own opinion.

Rehoboams young Counsellors proved the overthrow of his Kingdome. 'Tis brave for youth in all things to bee discreet and sober minded. Three virtues they say are prime ornaments of youth, Modesty, Silence, and Obedience.

Ah! Young men, keep close in every action to this one principle, *viz.* in every action resolve to bee discreet and wise, rather than affectionate and singular.

I remember, that a young Gentleman of *Athens*, being to answer for his life, hired an Orator to make his defence, and it pleased him well at his first reading, but when the young man by often reading it, that hee might recite it publickly by heart, begun to grow weary and displeased with it, The Orator bid him consider that the
Judges

Judges and the people were to hear it but once; and then it was likely that they at the first instant might bee as well pleased as hee.

Ah! Young men, your leaning upon your selves, or upon others, will in the end bee bitternesse and vexation of spirit; Young men are very apt to lean on their own Wit, Wisdome, Arts, Parts, as old men are to lean on a staff to support them; (as the Hebrew Word signifies, that is rendred *Lean*, in that of *Prov.* 3. 5.) this hath been the bane of many a choice wit, the losse of many a brave Head, the ruine of many a subtile pate.

שען

Shagnan.

Ajax thought it was only for cowards and weaklings to lean upon the Lord for succour, not for him, whence hee was foiled; lean not to great parts, lean not to natural or acquired accomplishments; lest you lose them and your selves too. Leaning to natural, or moral excellencies, is the ready way to bee stript of all. *Babylon* that bore her self bold upon her high Towers, thick walls, and twenty years provision laid in for a siege, was surprized by *Cyrus*.

'Twas said of *Cæsar*, that hee received not his wounds from the swords of enemies, but from the hands of friends, that is, from trusting in them.

Ah! How many young men have been wounded, yea slain by trusting to their own understanding, their own abilities?

'T was an excellent saying of *Austin* (*in te stas, & non stas*) hee that stands upon his wn strength, shall never stand. A Creature, if, like a single drop, left to it self, it spends and wastes it self presently, but if like a drop in the fountain and Ocean of being, it hath abundance of security.

Ah! Young men, Young men, if you will needs be leaning, then lean upon precious Promises,

2 Pet. 1. 4
Psal. 27. 1

ies, lean up the Rock that is higher than your selves, lean upon the Lord Jesus Christ, as *John* did, who was the youngest of all th Disciples, and the most beloved of all the Disciples. *J he* leaned much, and Christ loved him much. O lean upon Christs Wisdome for Direction, lean upon his Power for Protection, lean upon (his Purse) his Fulness for Provision, lean upon his Eye for Approbation, lean upon his Righteousness for Justification, lean upon his Blood for Remission, lean upon his Merits for Salvation. As the young Vine without her Wall to support her, will fall and sink: So will you young men, without Christ puts under his everlasting arms to support you, and uphold you; therefore above all leanings, lean upon him: by leaning on him, you will engage him; by leaning on him, you will gain more honour than you can give; by leaning on him, you

John 21. 20. ch. 13. 23

Can. 8. 5.

may even command him, and make *him eternally yours*, &c.

3 Direction.

Thirdly, *If you would bee good betimes, if you would seek and serve the Lord in the Spring and morning of your daies, then take heed of flatterers, and flattery.* Ah! how many Young men might have been very good, who are now exceeding bad, by hearkening to flatterers, and affecting flattery? Flattery undid young *Rehoboam*, *Ahab*, *Herod*, *Nero*, *Alexander*, &c. Flatterers are soul-murderers, they are soul-undoers, they are like evil Chirurgions, that skin over the wound, but never heal it.

Anastatius the Emperours motto was (*mellitum venenum blanda oratio*) smooth talk proves often sweet Poyson; Flattery is the very Spring and Mother of all Impiety, it blows the Trumpet, and draws poor souls into rebellion against God, as *Sheba* drew *Israel* to rebel against *David*;

(marginal note: 1 King 12 and ch. 22 Act. 12. 22, 23, 24.)

David; it put our first Parents upon tasting the forbidden fruit; it put *Absolon* upon dethroning of his Father; it put *Haman* upon plotting the ruine of the Jews; it put *Corah, Dathan,* and *Abiram,* upon rebelling against *Moses*; it makes men call evil good, and good evil, darkness light, and light darkness, &c. it puts persons upon neglecting the means of Grace, upon undervaluing the means of Grace, and upon contemning the means of Grace; it puts men upon abasing God, slighting Christ, and vexing the Spirit, it unmans a man, it makes him call black white, and white black; it makes a man change Pearls, for Pebles, and Gold for Counters; it makes a man judge himself wise, when hee is foolish; knowing, when he is ignorant; Holy, when hee is Prophane; Free, when hee is a Prisoner; Rich, when hee is Poor; high, when hee is low; full, when hee is empty; happy, when hee is miserable.

The Flatterers told *Dyonysius* that his spittle was as sweet as hony. Rev. 3. 17, 18.

ferable. Ah! Young men, young men, take heed of Flatterers, they are the very worst of sinners, they are left of God, blinded by Satan, hardened in sin, and ripened for hell. God declares sadly against them, and that in his word, and in his works; in his word, as you may see by comparing these Scriptures together, *Deut.* 29. 18, 19, 20. *Psal.* 78. 36. *Psal.* 36. 1, 2. *Job* 17. 5. *Ezekiel* 12. 24. *Dan.* 11. 21, 32, 34. *Psa.* 12. 2, 3. *They speak vanity every one with his neighbour, with flattering lips, and with a double heart, do they speak. The Lord shall cut off all flattering lips, and the tongue that speaketh proud things:* And as God declares sadly against them in his Word, so hee hath declared terribly against them in his works, as you may runne and read in his judgements executed upon *Ahabs* flattering Prophets, and upon *Haman*, and upon *Daniels* (Princely) false Accusers, &c. And why then will not you

Karah, signifies any cutting off, either by death, or banishment, &c.

you stop your ears against those wretches, that the hand and heart of God is so much against?

Again, As God declares against them, so good men detest them, and declare against them, as you may see by comparing these Scriptures together, *Psal.* 5. 8, 9, 10. *Prov.* 2. 16. *Prov.* 7. 21. *Prov.* 28. 23. *Job* 32. 21, 22. 1 *Thes.* 2. 5, 20. *Prov.* 20. 19 *Meddle not with him that flattereth with his lips?* Why so? why, because a man that flattereth his Neighbour, spreadeth a net for his feet, *Prov.* 29. 5. The Hebrew word (*Mahhalik* from *hhalak*) that is here rendred *Flatterer*, signifies a *Smooth-boots*, a soft butter-spoken man, because flatterers use smooth, soft speeches. Also the word signifies *to divide*, because a flatterers tongue is divided from his heart. Flatterers have their nets, and those that give ear to them, will bee taken to their ruine. A lying tongue hat-

> A preacher in *Constantines* time, presumed to call the Emperor Saint to his face, but hee went away with a check, *Euseb. de vit. Const. l. 4.*

The Hebrew word דָּחָה *Dahhah, signifies such a violent forcing of one, as he cannot stand, it signifies to throw down, to drive on forwards till a man fall into destruction.*

Hof. 14. 8.

hateth those that are afflicted by it, *and a flattering mouth worketh ruine,* Prov. 26. ult. A flattering mouth ruines name, fame, estate, body, soul, life.

Valerian the *Roman* Emperour used to say (*Non acerba, sed blanda*) not bitter, but flattering words do all the mischief.

When *Alexander* the Great was hit with an Arrow in the siege of an *Indian* City, which would not heal, hee said to his Parasites, you say that I am *Jupiters* son, but this wound cries, that I am but a man.

Now shall good men detest them, and abhor them as they are the pest of pests, the plague of plagues, and will you own them, will you take pleasure in them, to your ruine here and hereafter? the Lord forbid. Oh say to all Flatterers, as hee to his Idols, *Get you hence, for what have I more to do with you?*

Nay, once more consider, that
not

not onely the good, but the bad, not onely the best, but (some of) the worst of men have manifested their detestation of Flatterers and Flattery.

Leo the Emperour used to say, (*occulti inimici pessimi*) a close enemy is farre worse than an open. When a Court Parasite praised *Sigismund* the Emperour above measure, the Emperour gave him a sound box on the ear.

When *Aristobulus* the Historian presented to *Alexander* the Great Book that hee had written of his glorious acts, wherein hee had flatteringly made him greater than he was; *Alexander* (after he had read the book) threw it into the River *Hydaspes*, and said to the Author, it were a good deed to throw thee after it.

When the Flatterers flattered *Antigonus*, hee cryed out (*mentiris, mentiris in gutture, Hæ virtutes non latent in me*) thou lyest, thou lyest in thy throat, these virtues

tues that thou speakest of; I have not in mee, but I am like a Leopard, that have ten black spots to one white.

Augustus Cæsar, and *Tiberius Cæsar*, were deadly enemies to Flatterers, insomuch that they would not bee called Lords by their own children.

A good Symbole is attributed to *Trebonianus Gallus*, viz. (*Nemo amicus idem & adulator*) no Flatterer can bee a true friend.

Aristippus (the Philosopher) seeing *Diogenes* washing of herbs for his Dinner, said, if *Diogenes* knew how to make use of Kings, hee need not live upon raw herbs, as hee doth; to which *Diogenes* replied, that if *Aristippus* could content himself with Herbs, hee need not to turn Spaniel, or to flatter King *Dionysius* for a meals meat.

Ah! Young men, young men, shall God, shall good men, shall bad men detest and declare against Flatterers, and Flattery, and will not

not you turn a deaf ear upon them, yea fly from them, as from a Serpent, and shun them as you would shun Hell it self? if you do not, the very Heathens but now cited, will rise in judgement against you.

Flatterers are the very worst of sinners. The Flatterers told *Cæsar*, that his freckles in his face, were like the starrs in the firmament; they bought and sold *Aurelius* the Emperour at pleasure. And *Augustus* complained when *Varrus* was dead, that hee had none now left that would deal plainly and faithfully with him.

So men may gain by Flattery, they will bee like *Harpalus*, who said (*Quod Regi placet, mihi placet*) that which pleaseth the King, pleaseth mee, when *Astyages* set his own Son before him to feed upon him:

O but let every young man say, (into whose hands this Treatise shall fall) *Quod Deo pla-*

placet mihi placet) that which pleaseth God, pleaseth mee.

I have been the longer upon this, out of love to young mens souls, who are so apt to be insnared in the Flatterers net ; if ever you would bee good in good earnest, you must abhor Flatterers as the first-born of the Devil, and as such as are most pernitious to mens happinesse both here and hereafter.

It is reported of one *Oramazes*, that hee had an enchanted Egge, in which (as hee boasted himself) hee had inclosed all the happiness of the World, but being broken, nothing was found in it but wind. *Flatterers are the greatest cheaters, the greatest deceivers in the world.*

They say of the *Crocodile*, that when hee hath killed a man, hee will weep over him, as if hee were sorry, and did repent for what hee had done; the Application is easie.

marginal note: Whilst an Asse is stroaked under the belly, you may lay on his back what burden you please.

4 Directi-

4 Direction.

Fourthly, *If you would bee good betimes, if you would seek and serve the Lord in the spring and morning of your daies, then take heed of engaged affections to the things of the world.*

The Young man in the Gospel took many a step towards Heaven; *All these things have I kept from my youth up, what lack I yet?* Christ makes a very fair offer to him in the next words, *Jesus said unto him, If thou wilt bee perfect, go and sell that thou hast, and give to the poor, and thou shalt have treasure in Heaven, and come and follow mee;* thou shalt have Heaven for Earth, a Sea for a drop, a Treasure for a mite, a Crown for a crum. I but the Young mans affections were strongly engaged to the things of the world; and therefore hee turns his back upon Christ, and goes away sorrowful, because hee had great possessions. O the madness, the folly of this young man, who to enjoy a little temporal

Mat. 19. 16--24.

Multi amando res noxias sunt miseri, habendo miseriores. August. in Psal. 26.

temporal felicity, hath bid an everlasting farewel to Christ and Glory, in that *Gen.* 13. 2. it is said, that *Abraham* was very rich in Cattel, in Silver, and in Gold; the Hebrew word (*Cabedh*) that is here rendred *Rich*, signifies heavy, it signifies a burden, to shew us, that riches are a heavy burden, and an hinderance many times to Heaven and happiness; and this young man in the Gospel found it so to his eternal undoing. Though the load-stone cannot draw the Iron when the Diamond is in presence, yet earthly possessions did draw this young mans soul away, when Christ the Pearl of price was present; the World is a silken net, and this young man found it so; the World is like Golden Fetters, and this young man found it so; the World is like sweet poison, and this young man found it so; for hee had drunk so large a draught of it, that there was no room in his soul for Christ or Heaven, for
Grace

They are dulce venenum, a sweet poison. Bern.

Young Men. 193

Grace, or Glory. Some say, that when the Serpent *Scytale* cannot overtake the flying Passenger, shee doth with her beautiful colours so astonish and amaze them, that they have no power to passe away, till shee have stung them; such a Serpent the World proved to the young man in the Gospel, it did so affect him and take him, so amaze him, and amuze him, that hee could not stir till it stung him to death.

When the Moon is fullest, it is furthest from the Sun; so the more men have of the World, the further (commonly) they are from God; and this the young man in the Gospel made good.

Many have ventured life and limb, and many a better thing, to gain the things of this world, and yet after all, they have got nothing at all. *Achans* golden wedge, proved a wedge to cleave him, and his garment, a garment to shrow'd him.

The whole world is circular,

If mony were thrown to the dogs, they would not so much as smell at it, the greater is their folly and madness, that will go to hell gates for it.

O the

the heart of a man is triangular, and wee know a circle cannot fill a triangle; yea, if it bee not filled with the three persons in Trinity, it will bee filled with the World, the Flesh, and the Devil. The World may bee resembled to the fruit that undid us all, which was fair to the sight, smooth in handling, sweet in taste, but deadly in effect and operation.

Ah! Young men, Young men, have none of you found it so?

The world in all it's bravery is no better than the Cities which *Solomon* gave to *Hiram*, which hee called *Cabul*, that is to say, displeasing -- or dirty; the world will afford nothing but trivial Flowers, surrounded with many Bryers: O the vanity! the uncertainty, the imperfection of all things below! if a man should weigh his pay, and his pains together, his miseries, and his pleasures together, his joyes, and his

1 Kings 9. 13

his sorrows together, his mercies, and his crosses together, his good daies, and his bad daies together, will hee not conclude vanity of vanity, and all is vanity?

It was a wise and Christian Speech of *Charls* the fifth, to the Duke of *Venice*, who when hee had shewed him the glory of his Princely Palace, and earthly Paradise, instead of admiring it, or him for it, onely returned him this grave and serious *memento*; (*Hæc sunt quæ faciunt invitos mori*) these are the things which make us unwilling to dye; it was a good saying of one to a great Lord (upon his shewing him his stately House, and pleasant Gardens;) Sir, you had need make sure of Heaven, or else when you dye, you will bee a very great loser.

In my other Treatises, you may read more of the vanity, insufficiency, impotency, mutability, uncertainty, and inconstancy of the world, and to them I refer you.

Ah! Young men, Young men, 'tis onely Heaven that is above all winds, storms, and tempests, nor hath God cast man out of Paradise for him to think to finde out another Paradise in this world; the main reason, why many young men dote upon the world, is, because they are not acquainted with a greater glory: Men ate Acorns till they were acquainted with the use of Wheat. The Woman had the Moon under her feet, when she was cloathed with the Sun, and had a Crown of twelve stars upon her head.

Rev. 12. 1

Ah! Young men; were you but cloathed with the Sunne of Righteousness, and had you a Crown set upon your heads, by the hand of Faith, you would have all the things of this World which are as low, bespotted, and mutable, as the Moon, under your feet; well young men, as ever you would bee good betimes, sit loose from the things of this world, bee no longer worshipers of this golden Calf and never let the World, that should bee but your servant, become your Lord; O let

Heb. 11. 24, 25, 26, 27, 35. ch. 10. 34.

let not the Devil and the world have more service for an ounce of gold, than Christ shall have for the Kingdome of Heaven!

Ah young men! the World and you must part, or Christ and you will never meet; *you cannot serve God and Mammon.* The two poles shall sooner meet, than the love of Christ, and the love of the World.

Mat. 6. 14

5 Direction.

Fifthly, *If you would bee good betimes, if you would know, seek and serve the Lord in the spring and morning of your youth, then take heed betimes of carnal reason, take heed of consulting with flesh and blood.*

Gal. 1. 15, 16.

Many a hopeful young man hath been undone temporally, and undone eternally, by hearkning to those evil counsellors.

Carnal Reason is an enemy, yea, an utter enemy, nay, it is not only an utter enemy, but it is enmity, yea, enmities, *Rom.* 8. 7. An enemy may bee reconciled, but

Cicero, a Heathen, could say, that man would not bee so wicked, and do so wickedly, were it not for his reason.

man out of Paradise for him to think to finde out another Paradise in this world; the main reason, why many young men dote upon the world, is, because they are not acquainted with a greater glory: Men ate Acorns till they were acquainted with the use of Wheat. The Woman had the Moon under her feet, when she was cloathed with the Sun, and had a Crown of twelve stars upon her head.

Rev. 12. 1

Ah! Young men; were you but cloathed with the Sunne of Righteousness, and had you a Crown set upon your heads, by the hand of Faith, you would have all the things of this World which are as low, bespotted, and mutable, as the Moon, under your feet; well young men, as ever you would bee good betimes, sit loose from the things of this world, bee no longer worshipers of this golden Calf and never let the World, that should bee but your servant, become your Lord; O

Heb. 11. 24,25,26, 27,35. ch. 10. 34.

Young Men.

let not the Devil and the world have more service for an ounce of gold, than Christ shall have for the Kingdome of Heaven!

Ah young men! the World and you must part, or Christ and you will never meet; *you cannot serve God and Mammon.* The two poles shall sooner meet, than the love of Christ, and the love of the World.

5 Direction.

Fifthly, *If you would bee good betimes, if you would know, seek and serve the Lord in the spring and morning of your youth, then take heed betimes of carnal reason, take heed of consulting with flesh and blood.*

Many a hopeful young man hath been undone temporally, and undone eternally, by hearkning to those evil counsellors.

Carnal Reason is an enemy, yea, an utter enemy, nay, it is not only an utter enemy, but it is enmity, yea, enmities, *Rom.* 8. 7. An enemy may bee reconciled, but

Mat. 6. 14

Gal. 1. 15, 16.

Cicero, a Heathen, could say, that man would not bee so wicked, and do so wickedly, were it not for his reason.

enmity can never bee reconciled. Carnal Reason is not onely averse, but it is utterly averse to all Goodnesse, it builds strong holds and syllogisms against the most glorious Gospel-truths, and accounts the pretious things of Christ as a strange thing; carnal Reason will make God and Gospel do homage to it; when carnal Reason is in the Throne, Christ and his Truths must all bow, or bee judged before its bar.

Ah! Young men, young men, as ever you would bee good betimes, stop your ears against all carnal reasonings within you; carnal Reason judges the choicest things of the Gospel to bee meer foolishnesse, it is purblinde, and cannot see how to make a right judgement of Christ, his Word, his waies, and yet will controul all.

If you are resolved to bee still scholars to this Master, then you must resolve to bee unhappy here, and

1 Cor. 1. 23

and miserable hereafter. But

It is safer and better for you to imitate those young men, who in the morning of their daies have graciously, wisely, and resolutely withstood those evil Counsellors; Carnal Reason, Flesh and Blood; *Joseph*, and *Moses*, *Daniel*, *Shadrach*, *Meshach*, and *Abednego*, all these in the Prime-rose of their youth were good, at turning the deaf ear to carnal counsel, and carnal Counsellors.

Gen. 39. 7, 8, 9, 10, 11 &c.
Heb. 11. 24, 25, 26.
Dan. 1.

Cassianus reports of a young man that had given himself up to a Christian life, and his Parents misliking that way, they wrote letters to him, to perswade him from it; and when hee knew there were letters come from them, hee would not open them, but threw them into the fire; this example is worth a following.

Another famous example you have in the story of King *Edward* the sixth, when *Cranmer* and *Ridly* came to him, and were very earnest to have him give way to to his Sister the Lady *Mary* to have Masse; hee stood out and pleaded the case with them, that it was a sin against God, and provoking to the eyes of his glory, &c. but they still continued to use many carnal Arguments to perswade the King (who was but a childe about fifteen years of age) but hee withstood them a great while, but at length when hee saw hee could not prevail with all his pleading against those grave men, but that they still continued their sute, hee burst out into bitter weeping, and sobing, desiring them to desist; the motioners seeing his zeal and constancy, wept as fast as hee, and being overcome, they went away, and told one, that the King had more divinity in his little finger, than they had in all their bodies.

Ah! young men, it will be your safety, and your glory, to write after this Princely Copy, when you are surrounded with carnal reason, and carnal counsellors, &c.

Sixthly,

6 Direction.

Sixthly, and Lastly, *If you would bee good betimes, then take heed of comparing your selves with those that are worse than your selves.*

Young men are very apt to compare themselves with those that are worse than themselves, and this proves a snare unto them, yea, oftentimes their bane, their ruine; As it did the young Pharisee in the Gospel, who pleaded his negative Righteousness, hee was not as other men are, Extortioners, Unjust, Adulterers, and stood on his comparative goodness, nor as this Publican, hee stands not only upon his comparisons, but upon his disparisons, being blind at home, and too quick sighted abroad; hee contemneth and condemneth the poor Publican, who was better than himself, making good that saying of *Seneca*, the nature of man, saith hee, is very apt (*utimur perspicillis magis quam speculis*) to use spectacles to behold other mens faults, rather than

Joh. 9. 39, 40.

Luke 18. 11,12,13, 14
Thales, one of the seven sages, being asked what was the easiest thing in the world to do, answered, to know other mens faults, and none of our own.

than looking-glasses to behold our own; such Pharisees do justly incur the censure which that sowre Philosopher past upon Grammarians, that they were better acquainted with the evil of *Ulysses*, than with their own.

Diogenes apud Laertium. l. 6

Ah! Young man, young man, you know, hee that drinks poison, though hee drinks not so much as another; and hee that commits treason, though not so great, so high treason as another, shall yet as certainly bee poisoned, and hanged, as hee that hath drunk a greater quantity of poison, and committed higher acts of treason.

Matth. 11. 22, 23, 24, 25.
As in heaven, one is more glorious than another, so in hell, one shall bee more miserable than another. *Aug.*

Sirs, do not delude and befool your own souls, if you are not as wicked as others, you shall not bee as much tormented as others, but yet you shall bee as certainly damned as others, you shall as certain to Hell as others, you shall as sure bee shut out for ever from God, Christ, Saints, Angels, and all the Treasures,
plea-

pleasures, and glories of Heaven, as others, except it bee prevented, by timely repentance on your side, and pardoning mercy on Gods. Wilt thou count it madness, O young man! in him that is sick, to reason thus? I am not so sick, as such and such, and therefore I will not send to the Physician; And in the wounded man to say, I am not so desperately wounded as such and such, and therefore I will not send to the Chirurgion; and in the traitor to say, I am not guilty of so many foul and hainous treasons as such and such, and therefore I will not look after a pardon; and in the necessitous man to say, I am not so hard put to it as such and such, and therefore I will not welcome a hand of charity? and wilt thou not count it the greatest madnesse in the world for thee to put off thy repentance, and thy returning to the Lord in the spring and morning of thy youth, because that thou art not as sinful

as

as wicked as such and such, if to have a softer bed, a milder punishment in hell, than others, will satisfie thee, then go on; but if thou art afraid of the worm that never dyes, and of the fire that never goes out; being like that stone in *Arcadia*, which being once kindled, could not bee quenched; O then begin to bee good betimes! O seek and serve the Lord in the spring and morning of your daies!

Chrysost. Hom. 4. in Mat.

To think often of Hell, is the way to bee preserved from falling into Hell. Ah! young men, young men, that you would often consider of the bitterness of the damneds torments, and of the pittilesness of their torments, and of the diversity of their torments, and of the easelesness of their torments, and of the remedilesness of their torments. (*Momentaneum est quod delectat, Æternum quod cruciat.*) The sinners delight here is momentany, that which torments hereafter is perpetual; when a

Sinner

Sinner is in Hell, dost thou think, O young man! that another Christ shall bee found to dye for him, or that the same Christ will bee crucified again for him, or that another Gospel should be preached to him? Surely no.

Ah! Why then wilt thou not betimes return and seek out after the things that belong to thy everlasting peace? I have read of Pope *Clement* the fifth, that when a young Nephew of his died, hee sent his Chaplain to a Necromancer, to know of him how it fared with him in the other world, the Conjurer shewed him to the Chaplain, lying in a fiery bed in Hell, which when the Pope understood, he never joyed more, &c.

Jac. Rev. Hist. Pont. Rom. 199.

Ah! Young man, that these occasional hints of Hell, may bee a means to preserve thee from lying in those everlasting flames.

Bellarmine tells us of a certain advocate of the Court of *Rome*, that

Bellar. de arte moriendi, l. 2. c. 10

that being at the point of death, was stirred up by them that stood by, to repent and call upon God for mercy, hee with a constant countenance, and without sign of fear, turned his speech to God, and said, Lord, I have a desire to speak unto thee, not for my self, but for my Wife and Children, for I am hastening to Hell, neither is there any thing that thou shouldest do for mee; and this hee spake, saith *Bellarmine* (who was present, and heard it) as if hee had spoken of a journey to some Village or Town, and was no more affrighted.

Sir *Francis Bacon* also in his History of *Henry* the seventh, relates, how it was a common by-word of the Lord *Cordes*, that he would be content to lie seven years in hell, so hee might win *Calice* from the *English*; but if thou O young man art given up to such desperate Atheism, and carnal Apprehensions of hell, I am affraid God will confute thee one day by fire and brimstone; but I would willingly hope

hope better things of all those young persons, into whose hands this Treatise shall fall; and thus you see what things must bee declined and avoided; if ever you would bee good betimes, if ever you would seek and serve the Lord in the spring and morning of your daies.

CHAP. VII.

BUt in the second place, *as those things must be declined, so other things must carefully and diligently bee practised, if ever you would bee good betimes.* I shall instance onely in those that are most considerable and weighty; As

First, *If ever you would bee good betimes, &c. then you must labour to bee acquainted with four things betimes.*

1 Duty.

First, *You must labour to acquaint your selves with the Scripture betimes,* you must study the Word betimes; *David* studied the Word
in

Psal. 119. 97, 98, 99, 100, 101, 102, 103.

in the morning of his daies, in the prim-rose of his youth, and this made him wiser than his enemies, yea, than his teachers; this made him as much excel the antients, as the Sun excels the Moon, or as the Moon excels the twinckling Stars. *Timothy* was good betimes, and no wonder, for in the prime-rose of his daies, hee was acquainted with the Scripture, hee was inured to the Word from his child-hood, yea, from his infancy, as the Word properly signifies; so in that 119 *Psalm*, the 9. v. *Wherewithall shall a young man cleanse his way? by taking heed according to thy Word*; there is no way to a holy heart, and a clean life, but by acquainting of your selves with the Word betimes; one hath long since observed, that God hath bowed down the Scriptures to the capacity even of babes and sucklings, that all excuse may bee taken away, and that young men may bee encouraged to study the Scrip-

2 Tim. 3. 15. ἀπὸ βρέ-φοις. from a suckling.

Aug.

Young Men.

Scripture betimes. Ah! Young men, no Histories are comparable to the Histories of the Scriptures. 1. For Antiquity. 2. Rarity. 3. Variety. 4. Brevity. 5. Perspicuity. 6. Harmony. 7. Verity. All other Books cannot equal Gods, either in age, or authority, in dignity or excellency, in sufficiency, or glory.

Moses is found more antient and more honourable, than all those whom the *Grecians* make most antient and honourable, as *Homer*, *Hesiod*, and *Jupiter* himself, whom the *Greeks* have seated in the top of their divinity.

The whole Scripture is but one entire Love-letter, dispatcht from the Lord Christ to his beloved Spouse, and who then but would still bee a reading in this Love-letter? Like *Cæcilia* a *Roman* Maiden of Noble Parentage, who carried alwaies about her the New Testament, that shee might

Adoro Plenitudinem Scripturarum, Tertullian.

Gregory calls the Scripture (Cor & animam Dei) the heart and soul of God.

might still bee a reading in Christs Love-letter, and behold the sweet workings of his love, and heart, towards his dear and precious ones.

Luther found so much sweetness in the word, in Christs Love-letter, that made him say, he would not live in Paradise if hee might, without the word (*at cum verbo etiam in inferno facile est vivere*) but with the word he could live in hell it self.

The word is like the stone *Garamantides*, that hath drops of Gold in it self, enriching of the beleeving soul. This the Martyrs found, which made them willing to give a load of hay for a few leaves of the Bible in *English*.

Augustine professeth that the sacred Scriptures were his whole delight.

Hier. Epistola ad Heliod. in Epitaphium Nepotiani.

And *Hierom* tells (us) of one *Nepotianus*, who by long and assiduous meditation on the holy Scriptures, had made his breasts the library of Jesus Christ. And

And *Rabbi Chija* in the *Jerusalem Talmud*, saith, that in his account, all the world is not of equal value with one word out of the Law. That which a Papist reports lyingly of their Sacrament of the Mass, *viz.* that there are as many mysteries in it, as there bee drops in the Sea, dust on the Earth, Angels in Heaven, Stars in the sky, Atomes in the Sunbeams, or sands on the Sea-shore, &c. may bee truly asserted of the holy Scriptures.

Oh the mysteries, the excellencies, the glories, that are in the word! Ah, no book to this book, none so useful, none so needful, none so delightful, none so necessary to make you happy, and to keep you happy as this. It is said of *Cæsar* (*major fuit cura Cæsari libellorum, quam purpuræ*) that hee had greater care of his books, than of his Royal Robes, for swimming thorow the waters to escape his enemies, hee carried his books in his hand above the waters, but lost his Robe; now what are *Cæsars* books to Gods books.

Psal. 119.

Ah! Young men, young men, the Word of the Lord is a light to guide you; a Counsellor, to counsel you; a comforter, to comfort you; a staff, to support you; a sword, to defend you; and a Physician, to cure you; the word is a Mine, to enrich you; a Robe, to cloath you; and a Crown, to crown you; it is Bread, to strengthen you; and Wine, to cheer you; and a Hony-comb, to feast you, and Musick to delight you; and a Paradise, to entertain you.

The Jewish Rabbins were wont to say, that upon every letter of the law, there hangs mountains of profitable matter

Oh! Therefore before all, and above all, search the Scripture, study the Scripture, dwell on the Scripture, delight in the Scripture, treasure up the Scripture; no Wisdome, to Scripture Wisdome; no Knowledge, to Scripture Knowledge; no Experience, to Scripture Experience; no Comforts to Scripture Comforts; no
De-

Delights, to Scripture Delights; no Convictions, to Scripture Convictions; nor no Conversion, to Scripture Conversion.

Augustin hearing a voice from Heaven, that bad him take and read, whereupon turning open the New Testament, hee fell upon that place, *Let us walk honestly, as in the day, not in rioting and drunkennesse, not in chambering and wantonness, not in strife and envying. But put yee on the Lord Jesus Christ, and make not provision for the flesh, to fulfil the lusts thereof.* This Scripture so sunk into his heart, as that it proved the means of his conversion, as himself reports; this *Augustin* as hee was once preaching, his memory failing of him, contrary to his purpose, hee fell upon reproving the *Manicheans*, and by a Scripture, or two not before thought of; to confute their heresies, hee converted *Firmus* a *Manichaean*, as hee after acknowledged to *Augustin*, blessing God for that sermon.

Tolle & lege.

Rom. 13. 13, 14

Lib. 8. confes. cap. 11

Possidon de vita. Augustin.

It is reported of one *Adrianus*, who seeing the Martyrs suffer such grievous things in the cause of God, hee asked, what was that which caused them to suffer such things? and one of them named that Text; *Eye hath not seen, nor ear heard, neither hath it entred into the heart of man to conceive the things which God hath prepared for them that love him*: And this Text was set home, with such a power upon him, as that it converted him, and made him to profess Religion, and not onely to profess it, but to dye a Martyr for it.

Cyprian was converted by reading the Prophecy of *Jonah*. *Junius* was converted, by reading the first Chap. of *John* the Evangelist.

I have read of a scandalous Minister that was struck at the heart, and converted in reading that Scripture, *Thou which teachest another, teachest thou not thy self, &c?*

Wee read that *Paphnutius* converted *Thais* and *Ephran*, two famous

margin: 1 Cor. 2.9

margin: Rom. 2.21

Young Men.

mous strumpets, from uncleanness, onely with this Scripture-Argument, *That God seeth all things in the dark, when the doors are fast, the windows shut, the curtains drawn.* [Heb. 4.13.]

I have read of a poor man, who perswaded a young scholar to leave reading of Poetry, &c. and fall upon reading of the Scripture, which accordingly hee did; and it pleased the Lord, before hee had read out *Genesis*, to change his heart, and to turn him to the Lord in the Prime-rose of his daies, hee being then but twenty years of age.

I have read of a young Lady, called *Potamia*, of a very illustrious family, who endured very much in her Martyrdome, by the extream cruelty of *Basilides* her executioner, yet after her death, hee bethinking himself of the holy words, and Scripture-expressions that were uttered by her, during her cruel Torments, became a Christian, and within [Origen was her Schoolmaster.]

P 4 few

few daies after, was himself likewise crowned with Martyrdome.

James Andreas, a godly Minister, hearing of a Jew, that for Theft was hanged by the heels, with his head downward, having not seen that kinde of punishment, hee went to the place where hee was hanging between two Doggs that were alwaies snatching at him to eat his flesh, the poor wretch repeated in Hebrew some verses of the *Psalms*, wherein hee cryed to God for mercy, whereupon *Andreas* went near to him, and instructed him in the Principles of Christian Religion, about Christ the *Messiah*, &c. Exhorting him to beleeve in him, and it pleased God so to blesse his Scripture Exhortations to him, that the Doggs gave over tearing of his flesh, and the poor Jew desired him to procure, that hee might bee taken down and baptized, and hung by the neck for the quicker dispatch

A miracle of mercy.

patch, which was done accordingly.

I might produce other instances, but let these suffice to provoak all young persons to a speedy, serious, diligent, and constant study of the Scripture. Ah Sirs! you do not know how soon your blinde minds may bee enlightned, your hard hearts softned, your proud spirits humbled, your sinful natures changed, your defiled consciences purged, your distempered affections regulated, and your poor souls saved, by searching into the Scriptures, by reading the Scripture, and by pondering upon the Scripture; you should lay up the Manna of Gods Word in your hearts, as *Moses* laid up the Manna in the golden pot. And as *Tamar* did with the staff and signet that shee received from *Judah*, shee laid them up till shee came to save her life, and did save her life by it, as you may see in holy story.
The

Much in the word is wrap'd up in a little. It is more to bee admired, than to have Homers Iliads comprized in a Nut shell. Heb. 9. 4

Gen. 38. 18, -- 36

The laying up of the word now, may be the saving of your souls another day.

I have read of little Bees, that when they go out in stormy weather, they will carry a little of their comb, or gravel with them, that they may bee ballanced, and not carried away with the wind.

Ah! young men, young men, you had need to have your thoughts and hearts ballanced with the precious word, that you may not bee carried away with every wind of doctrine, as many have been in these daies, to their destruction and confusion.

Narcissus a beautiful youth, though hee would not love them that loved him, yet afterwards fell in love with his own shadow: Ah! how many young men in these daies, who were once lovely and hopeful, are now fallen in love with their own and others shadows, with high, empty, aiery notions, and with strange monstrous speculations to their own damnation?

2 Thes. 2. 10, 11, 12.

Ho-

Holy *Melancthon*, being newly converted, thought it impossible for his hearers to withstand the evidence of the Gospel, but soon after, hee complained that old *Adam* was too hard for young *Melancthon*.

Ah! young men, young men, if you do not in good earnest give up your selves to the reading, to the studying, to the pondering, to the beleeving, to the affecting, to the applying, and to the living up to the Scripture, Satan will bee too hard for you, the world will bee too hard for you, your lusts will bee too hard for you, temptations will bee too hard for you, and deceivers will bee too hard for you, and in the end you will bee miserable; and thus much for the first thing, &c.

2 Duty.

Secondly, *If you would bee good betimes, then you must acquaint your*

your selves with your selves betimes.

If you would bee gracious in the spring and morning of your daies, then you must see betimes how bad you are; how vile, how sinful, how wretched you are; no man beginnes to bee good, till hee sees himself to bee bad; the young Prodigal never beganne to mend, hee never thought of returning to his Father, till hee came to himself, till hee beganne to return into his own soul, and saw himself in an undone condition.

Luke 15. 12, — 22

Ah! Young men, Young men, you must see your selves *To bee children of wrath, to bee Enemies, to bee Strangers, to bee afarre off from God, from Christ, from the Covenant, from Heaven, to bee Sins servants, and Satans bond-slaves;* the ready way to bee found, is to see your selves lost; the first step to mercy, is to see your misery; the first step towards Heaven, is to see your selves neer to Hell; you won't look after

Eph. 2. 1. 2,3,12,13 Rom.6.16 Joh.8.44. 2 Tim. 2. 26.

...ter the Physician of souls, you won't prize the Physician of souls, you won't desire the Physician of souls, you won't match with the Physician of souls, you won't fall in love, in league with the Physician of souls, you won't resign up your selves to the Physician of souls, till you come to see your wounds, till you come to feel your diseases, till you see the tokens, the plague sores of divine wrath and displeasure upon you; as the whole do not need the Physician, so they do not desire, they do not care for the Physician.

Austin saith, hee would willingly go thorow Hell to Christ, so will all that see their need of Christ.

Ah! Young men, as you would bee good betimes, begin to acquaint your selves with your sinful selves betimes, beginne to acquaint your selves betimes with your natural and undone condition.

Zanche writ a Tractat, Quod nihil scitur.

There is a threefold self.

1 There is a natural self, as a mans parts, wit, reason, will, affections,

Affections, and Inclinations, &c.

2 A Religious self, and so a mans duties, graces, obedience, righteousness, holiness, are called ones self.

3 There is a sinful self, and so a mans corruptions, lusts, sinful nature and dispositions are called ones self; now if ever you would bee good betimes, you must acquaint your selves with your sinful selves betimes.

Demonicus being asked at what time hee beganne to bee a Philosopher: Answered, when I began to know my self. So a man never beginnes to bee a Christian, till hee begins to know himself. And indeed, for a man to know himself, to acquaint himself with himself, is one of the hardest works in all the World. For as the eye can see all things but it self, so most can discern all faults but their own. *Henry* the Fourth Emperor of *Germany*, his usual speech was (*Multi multa sciunt*

Luther said, that if a man could perfectly see his own faults, the sight therof would bee a very hell unto him.

sciunt, se autem nemo) many know much, but few know themselves.

The very Heathens did admire that saying as an Oracle (*osce te-ipsum*) know and bee acquainted with thy own self. The main exhortation of *Chilo*, one of the seven sages, was, know thy self; And *Plato* recordeth, that this saying of *Chilo*, know thy self, was written in letters of Gold, upon the Portal of *Apolloes* Temple.

Juvenal saith, that this saying, know thy self, came from Heaven. *Macrobius* saith, that the Oracle of *Apollo* being demanded what course should bee taken for attaining to felicity? answered, onely teach a man to know himself.

Thus you see, that both Divinity and Philosophy doth agree in this, that the best and surest way to true felicity, is, to know our selves, to acquaint our selves with our selves.

This

This Duty the Apostle charges upon the *Ephesians*, *Remember that you, being in times past Gentiles in the flesh, that at that time you were without Christ, aliens from the Common-wealth of Israel, and strangers from the Covenant of Promise, having no hope, and without God in the world.*

Here are five withouts, *without Christ, without the Church, without the Promise, without hope, and without God in the world.*

Man in his natural state is afar off, (hee is without) three manner of waies.

1 In point of opinion and apprehension.

2 In point of fellowship and communion.

3 In point of grace and conversion.

As you would be good betimes, dwell much upon your corrupt nature betimes; Ah! such is the corruption of our nature, that propound any divine good to it, it is entertained as fire by water, or

wet

Eph. 2.11, 12.
Of dull and insensible men, one long since thus complained (*patientius ferre Christi jacturam, quam suam*) that they did more calmly passe by the injuries done to Christ, than those that were done unto themselves

O the plague of unsensibleness!

wet Wood, with hissing; propound any evil, then it is like fire to straw, it is like the foolish Satyre, that made haste to kiss the fire; it is like that unctuous matter, which the naturalists say, sucks and snatches the fire to it, with which it is consumed; till you come to bee sensible of this, you will never begin to bee good, you will never look to have your hearts changed, and your souls saved.

The *Ethiopians* paint Angels black, and Devils white, in favour of their own complexion, and they say, that if the brute creatures could draw a picture of the Divine Nature, they would make their shape the Copy, and thus they flatter and delude themselves: take heed young men, take heed, that you do not put the like cheats upon your own souls, take heed that you bee not like those Limners, who so as they can make a mans Picture gay and gaudy, care not to draw it so as to resemble him, it is safest and best. O young man! to know the worst of thy self, and to know thy self, as thou art in thy self, and not as thy own flattering heart, or as other flatterers may represent thee to thy self.

3 Duty.

Thirdly, If you would bee good betimes; then *you must acquaint your selves with Jesus Christ betimes.*

You must know him betimes; A man never begins to bee good, till hee begins to know him that is the fountain of all goodness; *This is life eternal, to know thee, the onely true God, and Jesus Christ whom thou hast sent.*

The knowledge of Christ, is the beginning of eternal life, it is the way to eternal life, it is a taste of eternal life, it is a sure pledge and pawn to the soul of eternal life.

The *Spaniards* say of *Aquinas*, that hee that knows not him, knows not any thing, but hee that

John 17.3

that knows him, knows all things: hee that knows Jesus Christ, not notionally onely, but practically, not apprehensively onely, but affectively, hee knows all things that may make him happy; but hee that knows not Jesus Christ, knows nothing that will stand him in stead, when hee shall lye upon a dying bed, and stand before a judgement seat.

Justin Martyr relates, that when in his discourse with *Tryphon*, hee mentioned the knowledge of Christ, as conducing to our happiness and perfection, *Tryphons* friends laugh'd at it, but I hope better things of all those, into whose hands this treatise shall fall.

Sirs, the Sun is not more necessary to the world; the Eye to the body, the Pilate to the Ship, the General to the Army, &c. than the knowledge of Christ betimes, is necessary for all those that would bee good betimes.

Dear hearts, as ever you would bee good betimes, *you must labour*

bour, even as for life, *to know and bee thorowly acquainted with these six things*, concerning Jesus Christ, betimes.

First, If you would bee good betimes, then *you must know betimes, that there is every thing in Christ, that may encourage you to seek him, and serve him, to love him, and obey him, to beleeve on him, and to marry with him.*

If you look upon his names, his natures, his offices, his graces, his dignities, his excellencies, his royalties, his glories, his fulnesses, they all speak out as much.

Are you poor? why Christ hath tried gold to enrich you; are you naked? Christ hath white rayment to cloathe you; are you spiritually blinde? Christ hath eye-salve to enlighten you; are you in straights? hee hath wisdome to Counsel you; are you unrighteous? hee will bee righteousness to you; are you unholy? hee will bee holiness and sanctification to you; are you hungry?

Nec Christus, nec cœlum, patitur hyperbolen.

Rev. 3. 18

1 Cor. 1. 30.

Young Men. 226

gry? hee is bread to feed you; are you thirsty? hee is wine and milk to satisfie you; are you weary? he is a bed, a seat, to rest you; are you sick? why hee is a Physician to cure you, &c. (*Omne bonum in summo bono*) all good is in the chiefest good.

The Creatures have their particular goodness; health hath its particular goodness, and wealth hath its particular goodness, and learning hath its, and the favour of the Creature hath its, &c. but now Jesus Christ hee is an universal good, all the petty excellencies that are scattered abroad in the Creatures, are united to Christ; yea all the whole volume of perfections, which is spread through Heaven and Earth, is epitomized in him. *Ipse unus erit tibi omnia, qui in ipso uno bono, bona sunt omnia. Aug.* One Christ will bee to thee instead of all things else, because in him are all good things to bee found. *Abrahams* servant brought forth Jewels

Q 3

John 6.48
Isa. 55. 1
Mat. 11. 28
Mat. 9. 12

Christ is the *Bonum in quo omnia bona.*

Gen. 24. 53

els of Silver, and Jewels of Gold, to win *Rebeccah's* heart to *Isaac*; so should you, O young men! bee often in presenting to your own view, all those amiable and excellent things that bee in Christ, to win your hearts over to Christ betimes.

Secondly, If you would bee good betimes, *Then you must know betimes, that Jesus Christ is mighty to save.*

Heb. 7. 25
εἰς τὸ παντελὲς.
Perpetually.
Constantly.
Mat. 9. 28.
Isa. 63. 1
Mighty to save.

Hee is able to save to the uttermost, all them that come unto him, that beleeve in him, and that cast themselves upon him. The Lord hath laid help upon one that is mighty, Christ saves perfectly, thorowly, perpetually, them that come unto him.

The three tongues that were written upon the Cross, in Greek, Latin, and Hebrew, to witnesse Christ to bee the King of the *Jews*, do each of them in their several Ideoms avouch this Axiome, that Christ is an all-sufficient Saviour; and a three-
fold

fold cord is not easily broken. They say it is true of the Oyl at *Rhemes*, that though it bee continually spent in the auguration of their Kings of *France*, yet it never wasteth; Christ is that pot of Mannah, that cruse of Oyl, that bottomeless Ocean, that never fails his people; there is in Christ an all-sufficiency, for all Creatures, at all times, in all places.

 The great *Cham* is said to have a tree full of pearls, hanging by clusters, but what is the Great *Chams* tree, to Christ our tree of Life, who hath all variety and plenty of fruit upon him; the happiness that comes to beleevers by Christ are so many, that they cannot bee numbred, so great, that they cannot bee measured, so copious, that they cannot be defined, so precious, that they cannot bee valued; all which speaks out the fulness and all-sufficiency of Christ.

 There is in Christ (*plenitudo a-bun-*

Christ is never vacuis manibus, empty handed.

Rev. 22. 2 Christ is like the trees of the sanctuary, which were both for meat, and for medicine. Ezek. 47. 12

bundantia, and *plenitudo redundantia*) a fulness of abundance, and a fulness of redundancy, as well as a fulness of sufficiency.

There is in Christ,
1 The fulness of the Spirit.
2 The fulness of Grace.
3 The fulness of the Image of God.
4 The fulness of the God-head.
5 The fulness of Glory.

But I must not now open, nor dilate on these things, lest I should tire both my self, and the Reader.

Plutarch in the Life of *Phocion*, tells us of a certain Gentlewoman of *Ionia*, who shewed the wife of *Phocion*, all the rich Jewels, and precious stones shee had; shee answered her again, all my riches and Jewels is my husband *Phocion*; so may a penitent sinner say of his blessed Saviour, Christ is all my Jewels, my Riches, my Treasures, my Pleasures, &c. his sufficiency is all these, and more

more than these to mee.

The *Spanish* Ambassadour comming to see the treasury of Saint *Mark* (in *Venice*) which is cryed up thorow-out the World, fell a groping to finde whether it had any bottome, and being asked why, answered, In this amongst other things, my great Masters Treasure differs from yours, in that his hath no bottome, as I finde yours to have, alluding to the Mines in *Mexico*, and *Potosy*; but what are the *Spaniards* Treasures to Christs Treasures? a man may without much groping finde the bottome of all earthly Treasures, but who can finde the bottome of Christs treasures? should all created excellencies meet in one glorified breast, yet they could not inable that glorious God-like Creature to sound the bottome of those riches and treasures which are in Christ. *Ephes.* 3. 8. All which speaks out Christs all-sufficiency; and thus much for the second thing. Thirdly,

Ipse Deus sufficit ad præmium. Bern.

Thirdly, If you would bee good betimes, *Then you must know betimes, that there is a marvellous willingness and readiness in Christ, to embrace, to entertain, to welcome returning sinners, and to shew mercy and favour to them.*

The Young Prodigal did but think of returning to his Father, and hee ran and met him, and instead of kicking or killing him, hee kist him, and embrac'd him, his bowels rolled within him, and his compassions flowed out freely to him. *Ho every one that thirsteth, come yee to the waters, and hee that hath no mony, come yee, buy, and eat, yea, come buy wine and milk, without money and without price.* Nazianzen improveth this place thus; Oh this easie way of contract, hee giveth more willingly than others sell, if thou wilt but accept, that is all the price; though you have no merits, though you have nothing in your selves to incourage you, yet will you accept? If you

Luk. 15. 20, 21, 22

Isa. 55. 1 The meaning is, sell thy self, thine own wit, reason, self-worth, and that is all Christ desires, saith *Augustin* upon the words.

Young Men.

you will, all is freely yours; the waters shall bee yours, to cleanse you, and the milk yours, to nourish you, and the bread yours, to strengthen you, and the Wine yours, to comfort you; here poor Sinners are called three times to come; come faith Christ, come, come, to shew how marvellous, ready and willing hee is, that poor sinners should taste of Gospel delicates, so in that *John 7. 37: Jesus stood and cryed, if any man thirst, let him come to mee and drink.* So in that *Rev. 22. 17. Let him that is a thirst come, and whosoever will, let him take the water of life freely;* so in that *Rev. 3. 20. Behold, I stand at the door and knock, if any man hear my voice, and open the door, I will come in to him, and will sup with him, and hee with mee;* and so in that *Luke 14. 21. The Master of the house said to his servant, go out quickly into the streets, and lanes of the City, and bring in hither the poor, and the maimed, and the halt, and the*

Cant. 2. 8 Christ comes leaping upon the Mountains, and skipping upon the hills, to shew his readiness and willingness to do good to souls.

the blinde. Here is no man of quality, of dignity, of worldly Pomp or Glory, or of any self-sufficiency, that is invited to the feast, but a company of poor ragged, deformed, slighted, neglected, impoverished, wounded sinners; these are invited to feast with Christ.

Concerning this willingnesse of Christ, I shall speak more when I come to deal with Old sinners, in the cloze of this discourse, and to that I refer you, for further and fuller satisfaction, concerning the great readiness and willingness of Jesus Christ to entertain returning Sinners.

Fourthly, If you would bee good betime, *Then you must know betimes, that Jesus Christ is designed, sealed, and appointed by the Father, to the office of a Mediatour,*

Labour not for the meat which perisheth, but for that meat which endureth to everlasting life, which the Son

---

John 6.27 The Father sealed, even God, so the Greek hath it.

Son of man shall give unto you, for him hath God the Father sealed: God the Father hath made Chrifts commiffion authentical, as men do theirs by their feal. It is a Metaphor, a fimile taken from them who give Commiffions under hand and feal. God the Father hath given it under his hand and feal, That Jefus Chrift is the only perfon that he hath appointed, and fealed, allowed, and confirmed to the office of our redemption. If Jefus Chrift were never fo able to fave, and never fo willing, and ready to fave poor finners, yet if hee were not appointed, defigned, and fealed, for that work, the awakened Sinner would never look out after him, nor defire union with him, nor intereft in him; and therefore it is of very great confequence to know, that God the Father hath fent and fealed Chrift to bee a Saviour to his people, him hath God the Father fealed; Sealed by way of deftination, and fealed by way of of qualification, sealed by his Doctrine, sealed by his miracles, sealed by his Baptism, sealed by his Resurrection, but above all, sealed by his glorious unction. *The Spirit of the Lord is upon mee, because the Lord hath anointed mee to preach good tydings unto the meek; hee hath sent mee to binde up the broken hearted, to proclaim liberty to the captives, and the opening of the Prison to them that are bound.* To proclaim the acceptable year of the Lord, and the day of vengeance of our God; to comfort all that mourn, to appoint unto them that mourn in *Zion*, to give unto them beauty for ashes, the Oyl of joy for mourning, the garment of praise for the spirit of heaviness, that they might bee called trees of Righteousness, the planting of the Lord, that hee might bee glorified, neither Saints, nor Angels, are sealed and anointed to the great work of redemption, but the Lord Jesus us; you should alwaies look upon the Lord

---

Marginal notes:

Isa. 61. 1, 2, 3
Luk. 4. 18
Christ was anointed of God,
1 By way of designation. 2 By way of qualification. 3 By way of inauguration
This anointing was ordinarily used in the installing men to offices of any eminence.

Young Men. 339

Lord Jesus as sealed and anointed to the Office of a Mediatour, and accordingly plead with him.

Ah Lord! It is thy office, as thou art a sealed and an anointed Saviour and Redeemer, to subdue my sins, to change my nature, to sanctifie my heart, to reform my life, and to save my soul; and therefore do it for thy names sake; O do it for thy Office sake, do it for thy glories sake.

Thou art anointed with the Oyl of gladness above thy fellows; Thou hast a larger effusion of the Spirit upon thee, than others; thou art anointed with the Holy Ghost, and with power after an extraordinary measure and manner, thou art indued with all Heroical Gifts and Excellencies, plentifully, abundantly, transcendently, thou art sealed and predestinated; thou art invested into this office of Mediatorship under the Fathers hand and

Psa. 45.8
Act. 4.27

Act. 10.8

Iohn 1.16
Iohn 3.34

and seal; and therefore whither should I go for salvation, for remission, for redemption, for grace, for glory, but to thee?

Fifthly, If you would bee good betimes, *then you must know betimes, that there is no way to salvation, but by Jesus Christ.*

Neither is there salvation in any other (speaking of Christ) for there is none other name under Heaven, given among men, whereby wee must be saved; if ever you are saved, you must bee saved by him, and him onely, you must not look for another Saviour, nor you must not look for a co-saviour, you must bee saved wholly by Christ, and onely by Christ, or you shall never bee saved; you must cry out, as *Lambert* did (when hee was in the fire, and lifted up his hands, and fingers ends flaming) none but Christ, none but Christ. When *Augustus Cæsar* desired the Senate to joyn two Consuls with him for the better Government of the State, the

---

Marginalia:
Act. 4. 12 ἐν ἄλλῳ. that is, by or through the mediation of any other.

Act. and Mon.

Suetonius.

the Senate answered, that they held it as a diminution of his dignity, and a disparagement of their own judgement, to joyn any with so incomparable a man as *Augustus*.

Ah Friends! It is a diminution of Christs dignity, sufficiency, and glory, in the businesse of your salvation, to joyn any thing with the Lord Jesus, and it is the greatest disparagement in the world to your own judgements, knowledge, prudence, and wisdome, to yoak any with Christ in the work of Redemption, in the businesse of Salvation.

Augustin saith, that *Marcellina* hung Christs picture, and the picture of *Pithagoras* together; many there are, not only in *Rome*, but in *England* (yea, I am afraid in *London*) who joyn Christ and their works together, Christ and their Prayers together, Christ and their Teachers together, Christ and their mournings together

gether, Christ and their hearings together, Christ and their Alms together.

Ah! what a poor, what a weak, what an impotent, what an insufficient Saviour doth these men make Jesus Christ to bee? Except these men come off from these things, and come up onely to Jesus Christ, in the great business of salvation, they will as certainly, and as eternally perish (notwithstanding their hearing, knowing, and talking much of Christ) as those that never heard of Jesus Christ.

In the Old Testament, God commands them not to wear a Garment of divers sorts, as of woollen and linnen together, neither shall a Garment mingled of Linnen and Woollen come upon thee.

Deut. 22. 11. ch. 19. v. 19.

This Law was figurative, and shews us, that in the case of our Justification, Acceptation, and Salvation, wee are not to joyn our works, our services, with the

the Righteousness of Christ; God abhors a linsy-woolsey righteousness. And as by the Letter of this Law, in the Hebrews account, one threed of wool in a Linnen garment, or one Linnen threed in a woollen Garment, made it unlawful; So the least manner of mixture in the business of Justification, makes all null and void. And if by Grace, then it is no more of works; otherwise grace is no more grace: But if it bee of works, then it is no more grace; otherwise work is no more work; hee that shall mix his Righteousness with Christs, hee that shall mix his puddle with Christs purple blood, his rags, with Christs royal robes, his copper, with Christs gold, his water, with Christs wine, &c. is in the ready way to perish for ever.

On Earth Kings love no consorts, power is impatient of participation. Christ will bee *Alexander* or (*Nemo*) no body; hee wil l

Phil. 3. 9, 10.
Rev. 19. 8
Gal. 3. 28.
c. 2. 16.

Rom. 11. 6
Eph. 2. 5
Rom. 5. 15, 16, 18

will bee all in all in the businesse of Justification, or hee will bee nothing at all; wee must say of Christ, as it was once said of *Cæsar* (*socium habet neminem*) hee may have a companion, &c. but hee must not have a competitor.

Let us say of Christ, as the Heathen once said of his Petty gods (*contemno minutulos istos Deos, modo Jovem propitium habeam*) so long as hee had his *Jupiter* to friend, hee regarded them not; So, so long as wee have our Jesus to friend, and his Righteousnesse and Blood to friend, wee should contemn all other things, and abhor the bringing of any thing into competition with him; a real Christian cares not for any thing that hath not (*aliquid Christi*) something of Christ in it. Hee that holds not wholly with Christ, doth very shamefully neglect Christ, *Aut totum mecum tene, aut totum omitte,* saith *Gregory Nazianzen.*

margin: 1 Cor. 1. 30. Rom. 5. 19, 20.

Eph. 3. 9, 10 Psal. 71. 15, 16, 19. compared.

There

There is no other name, no other nature, no other blood, no other merits, no other person to bee justified and saved by, but Jesus Christ; you may run from Creature to Creature, and from Duty to Duty, and from Ordinance to Ordinance; and when you have wearied and tired out your selves in seeking ease and rest, satisfaction and remission, justification and salvation, in one way and another, you will bee forced after all to come to Christ, and to cry out, Ah! none but Christ, none but Christ. Ah! none to Christ, none to Christ, no works to Christ, no duties, no services to Christ, no prayers, no tears to Christ, no righteousness, no holiness to Christ. Well friends, remember this, that all the tears in the world cannot wipe off (meritoriously) one sin, nor all the Grace and Holinesse that is in Angels and men, buy out the pardon of the least transgression. All remission is only by

Isa. 55. 2
Rom. 10. 3

the

the Blood of Christ.

Sixthly and Lastly, If you would bee good betimes, *Then you must know betimes, that the heart of Jesus Christ is as much set upon sinners now hee is in Heaven, as ever it was when hee was upon Earth.*

Christ is no lesse loving, lesse mindful, lesse desirous of sinners eternal welfare now hee is in heaven (in a far Countrey) than hee was when hee lived on Earth: witnesse his continuing the Ministery of Reconciliation among poor Sinners in all ages; witnesse the constant treaties, that by his Ambassadors and Spirit hee still hath with poor sinners, about the things of their peace, the things of eternity; witnesse his continual knockings, his continual callings upon poor Sinners by his Word, Rod, Spirit, to open, to repent, to lay hold on mercy, and to be at peace with him; witnesse his continual wooing of poor sinners in the face of all neglects, and put-offs;

in

2 Cor. 5. 20

Rev. 3. 20
Isa. 56. 4
Isa. 27. 5

Cant. 5. 2, 3
Luke 14.

in the face of all delaies and denials; in the face of all harsh entertainment and churlish Answers; in the face of all gain-sayings and carnal reasonings; in the face of all the scorn and contempt that wretched sinners put upon him; and witness that plain word, *Jesus Christ, the same yesterday, and to day, and for ever.* Christ is the same aforetime, in time, and after time, hee is unchangeable in his essence, in his promises, and in his affections. *I am* Alpha *and* Omega, *the beginning and the ending, saith the Lord, which is, and which was, and which is to come.*

The Phrase is taken from the Greek Letters, whereof *Alpha* is the first, and *Omega* is the last; The first and last letter of the Greek Alphabet is a description of mee, saith Christ, who am before all, and after all, who am above all, and in all, who am unchangeable in my self, and in my thoughts and good will to poor sinners; Therefore do not

Prov. 6. 9
Mat. 22. 4.
23. 37

Heb. 13. 8

Rev. 1. 8.
11. ch. 21.
6. c. 22. 13.
It was a custome among the Turks, to cry out every morning from an high Tower, God alwaies was, and alwaies will be, and so salute their Mahomet.

poor souls, entertain any hard thoughts concerning Jesus Christ, as if hee was less mindful, less pittiful, and less merciful to poor souls now hee is in Heaven, than hee was when his abode was in this world.

And thus I have gone over those six things that you must know concerning Christ betimes, if ever you would bee good betimes. When Pope *Leo* lay upon his death-bed, Cardinal *Bembus* citing a text of Scripture to comfort him, hee replied (*Apage has nugas de Christo*) away with these bawbles concerning Christ; but I hope better things of you, and do desire that you will say of all things below this knowledge of Christ (that I have opened to you) as that devout Pilgrim, who travelling to *Jerusalem*, and by the way visiting many brave Cities, with their rare monuments, and meeting with many friendly entertainments, would often say, I must not stay here, this is not *Jerusalem*.

lem. Ah! so do you young men and women, in the midst of all your worldly delights and contents, cry out, Oh! wee must not stay here, this is not *Jerusalem*, this is not that knowledge of Christ that I must have, if ever I am happy here, and blessed hereafter.

4 Duty.

Fourthly and Lastly, *If you would be good betimes, then you must acquaint your selves with those that are good betimes.*

If you would bee gracious in the spring & morning of your youth, then you must begin betimes to be much in with them, who are much in with Christ, who lye near his heart, and know much of his mind: *Hee that walketh with wise men, shall bee wise, but a companion of fools, shall be destroyed,* or as the Hebrew hath it, shall bee broken in peeces, as when an Army is broken and routed by an enemy. (*Halech* from *Halech*) walking with the

Pro. 13. 20
ירוע
Shall bee broken, or shall bee worse, from רוע to bee naught.

'Twas the saying of one, as oft as I have been among wicked men, I return home lesse a man than I was before.

the wise, he shall be wise, for so the Original hath it; it is not talking with the wise, but walking with the wise, that will make you wise; it is not your commending, and praising of the wise, but your walking with the wise, that will make you wise; it is not your taking a few turns with the wise, that will make you wise, but your walking with the wise, that will make you wise; there is no getting much good by them that are good, but by making them your ordinary and constant companions.

Ah! Friends, you should do as *Joseph* in *Egypt*, of whom the Scripture saith, *Psal.* 105. 22. (according to the Hebrew phrase) that hee tied the Princes of *Pharaohs* Court about his heart.

If ever you would gain by the Saints, you must binde them upon your souls, you must labour to have very near, close, and intimate communion with them.

The Jews have a Proverb, that
two

two dry sticks put to a green one will kindle it; The best way to bee in a flame God-ward, Christ-ward, Heaven-ward, and Holiness-ward, is to bee among the dry sticks, the kindle-coals, the Saints: for as live coals kindle those that are dead; so lively Christians will heat and enliven those that are dead God-wards, Christ-wards, Heaven-wards, and Holiness-wards. As Iron sharpeneth Iron, so doth the face of a man his friend. *Prov. 27. 17*

Mens Wits, Parts, and Gifts, and industry, commonly grow more strong, vigorous, and quick, by friendly conference and communion.

And as hee that comes where sweet Spices and Oyntments are stirring, carries away a sweet favour with him; so hee that converseth with those that are good, shall carry away that goodness and sweetness with him, that shall render him sweet, desirable, and delectable to others.
Polemon

Polemon that *Augustin* speaks of, who was all for Wine and play, &c. became a brave man when hee came acquainted with the Philosophers School. So many young men, that have been all for Wine and Women, for playing and toying, for vanity and folly, have become brave men, precious men, by the company, counsel, and example of those who were gracious. Doctor *Taylor* the Martyr, rejoyced that ever hee came into Prison, because hee came thither to have acquaintance with that Angel of God, *John Bradford* (as hee calls him) so doubtless many young persons there bee that have much cause to rejoyce, and for ever to blesse the Lord, that ever they came acquainted with such and such (who fear the Lord, and who walk in his waies) for the good that they have received by them.

Algerius an *Italian* Martyr, said, hee had rather bee in prison

Au. Ep. 130

Young Men. 253

son with *Cato*, than with *Cæsar* in the Senate-house.

Ah young men! young men, you were better bee with the people of God, when they are in the lowest and most contemptible condition, than with the great (wicked) ones of the world, when they are in all their Royalty and Glory; in the day of account you will finde that they have made the best Market, who have rather chosen to keep company with *Lazarus*, though in his raggs, than they would (with others) keep company with *Dives*, though in his Purple Robes.

Well, young men, remember this, cloaths and company do oftentimes tell tales, in a mute, but significant language.

Tell mee with whom thou goest, and I will tell thee what thou art, saith the *Spanish* Proverb. *Cicero* (though a Heathen) had rather to have no companion, than a bad one: The Lord grant that this

Moses was of the same mind and metal Heb. 11. 24,25,26,27

Those that keep ill company, are like those that walk in the Sun, who are tann'd insensibly.

this Heathen (and others among them, that were of the same mind with him) may never rise up in judgement against any of you, into whose hands this Treatise may fall.

And thus I have dispatcht those four things that you must bee acquainted with betimes, (*viz.* the Scripture, your own hearts and conditions, the Lord Jesus Christ, and those that fear him) if ever you would bee good betimes.

Secondly, *If you would bee good betimes*, if you would seek and serve the Lord in the spring and morning of your daies, *Then you must shun the occasions of sin betimes*; A man will never begin to bee good, till he begin to decline those occasions that have made him bad, 1 *Thes.* 5. 22. *Abstain from all appearance of evil.*

Wee must shun (quicquid fuerit male coloratum) Whatsoever looks but ill-favouredly, as Bernard hath it.

You must shun and bee shie of the very appearance of sin, of the very shews and shadows of sin. The word εἶδος, which is ordinarily rendred *Appearance*, signifies

fies kind, or sort; and so the meaning of the Apostle seems to bee this, *Abstain from all sort, or the whole kind of evil*; from all, that is truly so, bee it never so small.

The least sin is dangerous; *Cæsar* was stab'd with Bodkins, and many have been eaten up of Mice, and Lice.

The least spark may consume the greatest house, the least leak may sink the greatest ship, the least sin is enough to undo thy soul, and therefore shun all the occasions that lead unto it.

Job made a Covenant with his eyes; *Joseph* would not bee in the room where his Mistress was; and *David* (when himself) would not sit with vain persons. As long as there is fuel in our hearts for a temptation, wee cannot bee secure; hee that hath Gun-powder about him, had need keep far enough off from sparkles; hee that is either tender of his credit abroad, or comfort at home, had need shun, and bee

shie

Job 31. 1.
Gen. 39. 10
Psa. 26. 3, 4, 5, 6, 7

shie of the very shew and shadow of sin; hee that would neither wound Conscience nor Credit, God, nor Gospel, had need hate the Garment spotted with the flesh.

In the Law, God commanded his people, not onely that they should worship no Idol, but that they should demolish all the monuments of them, and that they should make no covenant nor affinity with those who worshiped them, and all, left they should be drawn by these occasions to commit Idolatry with them; hee that would not taste of the forbidden fruit, must not so much as gaze on it; and hee that would not bee bit by the Serpent, must not so much as parley with the Serpent.

It is very observable, That in the Law, the Nazarite was not only commanded to abstain from wine and strong drink, but also hee might not eat Grapes, whether moist or dry, or any thing that

Jude 23. The sin and the coat of the sin is to be hated, saith Ambrose.

Latet anguis in herba. Snakes are found among roses. Numb. 6. 3, 4. Quid est vitare peccata, nisi vitare occasiones peccatorum? Melan.

that is made of the Vine-Tree; from the kernels, even to the husk; but why not these small things, in which there could bee no danger of Drunkenness? surely, lest by the contentment of these, hee might bee drawn to desire the Wine, and so bee brought on to sin, to break his vow (and so make work for Hell, or for the Physician of souls.) God hereby forbidding the most remote occasions, shews how wary and exactly careful men should bee, to shun, and avoid all occasions, provocations, and appearances of evil; and indeed, wee had need to keep off from slippery places, who can hardly stand fast on dry ground; hee that ventures upon the occasion of sinne, and then praies, *Lord, lead mee not into temptation*, is like him that thrusts his finger into the fire, and then praies that it may not bee burnt; or like him that is resolved to quench the fire with oyl, which in-

What is it to avoid sin, but to avoid the occasions of sin?

instead of quenching it, is as fuel to feed it, and encrease it. It was a notable saying of one, (*Majus est miraculum inter vehementes occasiones non cadere, quam mortuos suscitare*) It is a greater miracle not to fall, being among strong occasions, than it is to raise up the dead; hee that would not bee defiled, must not touch pitch; hee that would not bee burnt, must not carry fire in his bosome; hee that would not eat the Meat, must not meddle with the Broth; hee that would not fall into the pit, must not dance upon the brink; hee that would not feel the blow, must keep off from the Train; *keep thee far from a false matter*, Exod. 23. 7. Hee that will not flye from the occasions and allurements of sin (though they may seem never so pleasant to the eye, or sweet to the taste) shall finde them in the end to bee more sharp than Vinegar, more bitter than Worm-wood, more

Bernard in Cant. Serm. 65

Pro. 6. 27, 28, 29
Non diu tutus est, periculo proximus. Cypr. He is not long safe, that is near to danger.

more deadly than poison.

There is a great truth in that saying of the Son of *Syrach*, *Hee that loveth danger, shall perish therein; hee that will not decline danger, shall not bee able to decline destruction.* [Eccl. 3. 26, 27]

Socrates speaks of two young men that flung away their belts, when being in an Idol Temple, the lustrating water fell upon them, detesting (saith the Historian) the Garment spotted by the flesh! and will you, O young men, play and toy with the occasions of sin? the Lord forbid.

There are stories of several heathens that have shunned and avoided the occasions of sin, and will you dare to venture upon the occasions of sin?

Alexander would not see the woman after whom hee might have lusted.

Scipio Africanus warring in *Spain*, took New *Carthage* by storm, at which time a beautiful and noble Virgin fled to him

for

for succour to preserve her chastity, hee being but four and twenty years old (and so in the heat of youth) hearing of it, would not suffer her to come into his sight, for fear of temptation, but caused her to bee restored in safety to her Father.

Livia counselled her Husband *Augustus*, not onely not to do wrong, but not to seem to do so, &c.

Cæsar would not search *Pompeyes* Cabinet, lest hee should finde new matters of revenge.

Plato mounted upon his Horse, and judging himself a little moved with pride, did presently light from his Horse, lest hee should bee overtaken with loftinesse in rideing.

Theseus is said to cut off his golden locks, lest his enemies should take advantage by taking hold of them.

Ah! Young men, young men, shall the very Heathens thus shun and fly from the occasions of sin,

Aure. victor.

Dio. in vita.

sin, and will not you? will not you, who sit under the Sun-shine of the Gospel? these will in the great day of account bee sad and sore witnesses against those that dally and play with the occasions of sin.

To prevent carnal carefulness, Christ sends his Disciples to school, to the irrational creatures, *Mat.* 6. 26, -- 32. And to prevent your closing with the occasions of sin, let mee send you to school to the like creatures, that you may learn by them to shun and avoid the occasions of sin.

The *Sepiæ,* a certain kinde of fish, perceiving themselves in danger of taking, by an instinct which they have, they do darken the water; and so many times escape the net which is laid for them.

Geese (they say) when they fly over *Taurus*, they keep stones in their mouthes, lest by gagling, they should discover themselves to the Eagles, which are amongst the mountains waiting for them;

them; now if all these considerations put together, will not work you to decline the occasions of sin, I know not what will. There is a truth in that old saying,

Hee that will no evil do,
Must do nothing belongs thereto.

Exod. 22. 19.

The *Israelites* must have no leaven in their houses, till the Passover bee done, lest they should bee tempted to eat of it.

3 Direction.

Thirdly; *If you would be good betimes, then you must remember the eye of God betimes.*

Psa. 139. 2--14.

If you would seek and serve the Lord in the spring and morning of your daies, then you must study Gods omnipresence betimes.

Job 31. 4. ch. 34. 21, 22, &c.

Doth not hee see my waies, and count all my steps, for his eyes are upon the waies of man, and hee seeth all his goings? There is no darknesse, nor shadow of death, where the

workers

workers of iniquity may hide themselves.

I have read that *Paphnutius* converted two famous young strumpets, *Thais* and *Ephron*, from uncleanness, onely with this Argument, that God seeth all things in the dark, when the doors are fast, the windows shut, and the curtains drawn. By this very Argument *Solomon* labours to take off his Young man from carnal and sinful courses; *And why wilt thou my son bee ravish'd with a strange woman, and embrace the bosome of a stranger? for the waies of man are before the eyes of the Lord, and hee pondereth all his goings.* Thou may'st deceive all the world, like that counterfeit *Alexander* in *Josephus* his story, but *Augustus* will not bee deceived, hee hath quicker and sharper eyes.

Ah! Young men, young men, you may deceive this man, and that, and as easily deceive your selves, but you cannot deceive him, who is (πανόφθαλμος, *totus oculus*)

Non se putent adulteri noctis tenebris, vel parietum obtegi. Beda.

Pro. 5. 20, 21
Noli peccare, Deus videt, angeli astant, &c.
Take heed what thou doest, God beholds thee; Angels observe thee.

oculus) all-eye. As the eyes of a well-drawn picture are fastened upon thee, which way soever thou turnest, so are the eyes of the Lord. I have read of one, who being tempted to Adultery, said, they could not bee private enough, and being carried from room to room, answered, wee are not yet private enough, God is here.

Jer. 13. 27. ch. 29. 23

Ah Friends! his eyes which are ten thousand times brighter than the Sun, compasseth thy words, thy waies, thy works, thy thoughts, thy bed, thy board, thy bench. The *Egyptian* Hieroglyphick for God, was an eye on a Scepter, shewing that hee sees and rules all things.

Heb. 4. 13
Tetrachelismena.

Ah Friends! All Thoughts, Words, Hopes, and Hearts, are naked, opened, dissected and quartered before that God with whom you have to do. God is very curious and exact in marking and observing what is done by men, that hee may render to every man according to his works.

Au-

Augustin speaks of an old *Comædian*, when having no other spectators, went usually into the Theatre, and acted before the Statues of the Gods.

Ah! Young men and women, the eye of God should bee more to you, than all the world besides; O that the Scripture might bee written with the pen of a Diamond upon your hearts. *Hear yee not mee* (faith the Lord) *and will you not tremble at my presence?* There is a great truth in that saying of his (*Magna nobis ex hac indita est probitatis necessitas, quia omnia ante oculos judicis facimus cuncta cernentis.*) A great necessity of goodness is from hence put into us, because wee do all things before the eyes of a Judge, that sees all things.

4 Direction.

Fourthly, *If you would bee good betimes, then you must hearken to the voice of Conscience betimes.*

Aug. de civ. Dei. l. 6. c. 10.

Jer. 5. 21, 22.

Boetius de consol. l. 5.

2 Tim. 1. 3

A man will never begin to bee good, till hee begins to hearken to what Conscience speaks: So long as man turns a deaf ear to Conscience, hee is a safe Prisoner to Satan, and a sure enemy to good.

Psa. 58. 4
Joh. 3. 20, 21

Ah! how good might many have been, had they but begun betimes to hearken to Conscience?

Ah! Young men, do not dally with Conscience, do not play, do not trifle with Conscience, do not stop your ears against Conscience; hee that will not in his Youth give Conscience audience, shall at last bee forced to hear such lectures from Conscience, as shall make his life a very Hell. A sleepy Conscience, is like a sleepy Lion, when hee awakes, hee roars and tears, so will Conscience, *Mark* 9. 22. Conscience is (*mille testes*) a thousand witnesses for or against a man; hee that hath long turned the deaf ear to Conscience, shall at last

Such shall finde conscience to bee *Judex*, *index*, *vindex*.

finde

finde his Conscience like *Promotheus's vulture*, that lyes ever a gnawing. *Judas* found it so, and *Spira* found it so, and *Blaer* a great Counsellor of *Scotland*, found it so.

I have read of one *John Hofmeister*, that fell sick in his Inne, as hee was travelling towards *Auspurge* in *Germany*, and grew to that horror of Conscience, that they were fain to binde him in his bed with chains, where hee cryed out, that hee was for ever cast off by God, and that the promises that were set before him would do him no good, and all because hee had wounded his Conscience, and turned a deaf ear to Conscience.

Jo. Wolf. lect mem. To. 2. ad an. 1547

Well Young men, if you will not betimes hearken to Conscience, you shall at last hear Conscience saying to you, as the probationer Disciple said to Christ, *Master, I will follow thee whithersoever thou goest*; so saith Conscience, Sinner, I have called up-

Mat. 8.19

upon thee many a thousand times, and told thee, that I must by commission, bee thy best friend, or thy worst enemy; but thou wouldest not hear; and therefore now I will follow thee, whither ever thou goest; fast, and I will follow thee, and fill thee with horrours, and terrors; feast, and I will follow thee, and shew thee such a hand writing upon the wall, as shall cause thy countenance to change, thy thoughts to bee troubled, the joints of thy loins to bee loosed, and thy knees dashed one against another; stay at home, and I will follow thee, from bed to board; go abroad, and I will follow thee into all places and companies, and thou shalt know that it is an evil and a bitter thing, that thou hast so often and so long neglected my calls, and disobeyed my voice, and walkt contrary to mee; how thou shalt finde a truth in that saying of *Luther* (*una guttula malæ conscientiæ totum mare*, &c.) one drop of an evil Conscience swallows

Dan. 5. 5, 6
Tolle conscientiam, tolle omnia.
Take away conscience, and take away all, said the Heathen.

swallows up the whole Sea of worldly joy.

Well young men, There is a day a coming, wherein a good Conscience will bee better than a good purse, for then the Judge will not bee put off with a suite of Complements, or fair words, nor drawn aside with hope of reward; and therefore as you would bee able to hold up your heads in that day, make Conscience of hearkening to the voice of Conscience in this your day.

5 Direction.

Fifthly, *If you would bee good betimes, then you must know betimes wherein true happiness lies.*

For a man will never begin to bee good, till hee begins to understand wherin his happiness consists.

The Philosophers speaking of happiness, were divided into two hundred eighty eight opinions, every one intending something, and yet resolving nothing. Therefore the man in *Plutarch*, hearing

Quot homines, tot sententiæ, so many men; so many minds.

ing them wrangle about mans (*summum bonum*) chiefest good, one placing it in this, and another in that; hee went to the market, and bought up all that was good, hoping among all, hee should not miss of it, but hee did; many look for happiness in sin, others look for it in the Creatures, but they must all say, it is not in us (*Nil dat quod non habet*) nothing can give what it hath not; if the Conduit Pipe hath no water, it can give no water; if a man hath no money, he can give no money; if the Creatures have no happiness, they can give no happiness; Now this jewel, this pearl, happiness, is not to bee found in the breast, in the bosome of Creatures; in a word, because I must hasten to a close, mans happiness lies,

First, In his communion with God, as experience and Scripture demonstrates. Happy is that people, that is in such a case (but give mee that word again) yea happy is that people, whose God is the Lord.

Isa. 56. 12
Job 28. 14

Psa. 144. 15.

Lord. A man whose soul is in communion with God, shall finde more pleasure in a desert, in a dungeon, in a den, yea, in death, than in the Palace of a Prince, than in all worldly delights and contents, &c.

Secondly, In pardon of sin, *Blessed is hee whose transgression is forgiven, whose sinne is covered: Blessed is the man unto whom the Lord imputeth not iniquity, and in whose spirit there is no guile.* It is not, blessed is the honourable man, but, blessed is the pardoned man; It is not, blessed is the rich man, but, blessed is the pardoned man; It is not, blessed is the learned man, but, blessed is the pardoned man; It is not, blessed is the politick man, but, blessed is the pardoned man; It is not, blessed is the victorious man, but, blessed is the pardoned man; Do with mee what thou wilt, since thou hast pardoned my sins, saith *Luther*.

Psa. 32. 1, 2

Thirdly, In a compleat fruition and enjoyment of God, when wee shall bee here no more. *Bles-*

―sed are the pure in heart, for they shall see God. Now they see him but darkly, but in Heaven they shall see him face to face, they shall know as they are known; but of these things I have spoken largely elsewhere; and therefore shall satisfie my self with these hints.

6 Direction.

Lastly, *If you would bee good betimes, then you must break your covenant with sin betimes.*

You must fall out with your lusts betimes; you must arm and fence your selves against sin betimes; a man never begins to fall in with Christ, till hee begins to fall out with his sins; till sin and the soul bee two, Christ and the soul cannot bee one: *Now to work your hearts to this, you should alwaies look upon sin under these notions.*

1 Notion.

First, *If you would have the league dissolved betwixt sin and your souls betimes, then look upon sinne under the notion of an enemy betimes.*

Dearly

Mat. 5. 8
1 Cor. 13. 12.
Isa. 28. 15. 18.

Dearly beloved, I beseech you as strangers and Pilgrims, abstain from fleshly lusts, which war against the soul. As the Viper is killed by the young ones in her belly; so are poor sinners, betrayed and killed by their own lusts, that are nourished in their bosomes.

Pittacus, a Philosopher, challenging *Phlyon* the *Athenian* Captain (in their wars against them) to single combate, carried a net privily, and so caught him, and overcame him; So doth sin with poor sinners, the dangerous, pernicious, malignant nature of sinne; You may see in the story of the *Italian*, who first made his Enemy deny God, and then stabbed him to the heart, and so at once murdered both body and soul. Sin betraies us into the hand of the Devil, as *Dalilah* did *Sampson* into the hands of the *Philistims*.

Sugred poisons go down pleasantly; Oh! but when they are down

1 Pet. 2. 11
Sins, especially against knowledge (are *peccata vulnerantia & devastantia*.) wounding and wasting.

T

down, they gall and gnaw, and gripe the very heart-strings asunder, it is so with sinne; Ah! souls, have not you often found it so?

When *Phocas* the Murderer, thought to secure himself by building high walls, hee heard a voice from Heaven telling him, that though hee built his Bulwarks never so high, yet Sinne within would soon undermine all.

Ambrose reports of one *Theotimus*, that having a disease upon his body, the Physician told him, that except hee did abstain from intemperance, Drunkenness, Uncleanness, hee would lose his eyes; his heart was so desperately set upon his sins, that hee cries out, *(vale lumen amicum)* farewel sweet light.

Ah! how did his lusts war hot against body and soul?

The old man is like a Treacherous friend, and a friendly Traitour; though it bee a harde thing

thing to fight with a mans lusts, than it is to fight with the Cross; yet you must fight or dye, if you are not the death of your sinnes, they will prove the death of your soules.

The Oracle told the *Cyrrheans*, (*noctesq; diesq; balligerandum*) they could not bee happy, unless they waged warre night and day; no more can wee, except wee live and dye fighting against our lusts.

Ah! Young men, Can you look upon sin under the notion of an enemy, and not break with it, and not arm against it?

Well, remember this, the pleasure and sweetness that follows victory over sinne, is a thousand times beyond that seeming sweetness that is in sin; and as victory over sin is the sweetest victory, so it is the greatest victory; there is no conquest to that which is gotten over a mans own corruptions, *Hee that is slow to anger, is better*

As one of the Dukes of *Venice* died fighting against the Nauratines, with his weapons in his hand.

than the mighty, and hee that ruleth his spirit, than hee that taketh a City.

It is noble to overcome an enemy without, but it is more noble to overcome an enemy within; it is honourable to overcome fiery flames, but it is far more honourable to overcome fiery lusts.

When *Valentinian* the Emperor was upon his dying-bed, among all his victories only one comforted him, and that was victory over his worst enemy, *viz.* his own naughty heart.

Rom. 7.
22, 23
2 Cor. 10.
3, 4, 5, 6.
Gal. 5. 17.

Ah! Young men, young men, your worst enemies are within you, and all their plots, designs, and assaults are upon your souls, your most noble part; they know if that fort-Royal bee won, all is their own, and you are undone, and shall bee their slaves for ever; and therefore it stands you upon, to arm your selves against these inbred enemies; and if you ingage Christ in the quarrel, you will carry the day, and
when

when you shall lye upon your dying-beds, you will then finde that there is no comfort to that, which ariseth from the conquests of your own hearts, your own lusts.

2 Notion.

Secondly, *If you would break covenant with sin, if you would arm and fence your selves against sin betimes, then look upon sin as the souls bonds.* 2 Pet. 3. 6 Gal. 3. 10 Joh. 8. 34

For as bonds tye things together, so doth sin tye the sinner, and the curse together, it binds the sinner and wrath together, it links the sinner and Hell together. I perceive that thou art in the gall of bitterness, and in the bond of iniquity; iniquity is a chain, a bond, now bonds and chains gall the body, and so doth sin the soul, and as poor captives are held fast in their Chains, so are sinners in their Sins, they cannot redeem themselves by price, nor by power. 2 Tim. 2. ult.

Ah! Young men, young men,

Augustine saith of *Rome*, that shee was the great Mistress of the world, and the great drudge of sin.

no bondage to soul-bondage, no slavery to soul-slavery; the *Israelites* bondage under *Pharaoh*, and the Christians bondage under the *Turks*, is but the bondage of the body, of the baser and ignoble part of man, but yours is soul-bondage, soul-slavery, which is the saddest and greatest of all.

Ah Friends! You should never look upon your sins, but you should look upon them as your bonds, yea, as the worst bonds that ever were; all other Chains are golden Chains, Chains of Pearl, compared to those Chains of Iron and Brass; those chains of lusts, with which you are bound. Ah! who can thus look upon his chains, his sins, and not loathe them, and not labour for freedome from them? *Justinian* the Emperors Motto was (*Libertas res inestimabilis*) liberty is unvaluable; if civil liberty bee, surely spiritual liberty is much more; if you ask souls that were once in a state of bondage, but

are

are now Christs free-men, they will tell you so.

It was a good observation of *Chrysostome*, that *Joseph* was the free-man, and his Mistress was the servant, when shee was at the beck of her own lusts, when she tempted, and hee refused. Such as live most above sin and temptation, are the greatest free-men, others that live under the power of their lusts, are but slaves, and in bonds, though they dream and talk of freedome, *Tit.* 3. 3.

Chrysost. Hom. 19. in prior. Epist. ad Corinth.

3 Notion.

Thirdly, *If you would break league with sin, and arm and fence your selves against it, then look alwaies upon sin under the notion of fire.*

And others save with fear, pulling them out of the fire. Oh! snatch them out of their sins, as you would snatch a child, a friend, out of the fire; or as the Angel snatch'd *Lot* out of *Sodome*, hastily, and with a holy violence; natural fire may burn the house, the goods,

Jude 23. Arpazontes signifies a violent snatching; as the tender hearted mother to save the life of her child, pulls it hastily, and with violence out of the fire.

goods, the treasure, the servant, the childe, the wife, the body, but this fire burns the soul, it destroies and consumes that noble part, which is more worth than all the treasures of a thousand worlds; every man hath a hand, and a heart to quench the fire which burns his neighbours house, but few men have either hands or hearts to quench the fire that burns their neighbours souls, this is, and this shall bee for a lamentation.

D. Denisons three-fold resolution. par. 2. Sect. 2.

I have read of one, who upon the violence of any temptation to sin, would lay his hand upon burning coals, and being not able to abide it, would say to himself, Oh! how unable shall I bee to endure the pains of Hell? and this restrained him from evil; but what is the fire of Hell to the fire of sin? now to provoke you to look upon sin under the notion of Fire, consider with mee the sundry resemblances between material and immaterial fire, between corporal common fire, and between this

this spiritual fire, Sin. As,

First, Fire is terrible and dreadful; A ship on fire, an house on fire, Oh how dreadful is it? so sin set home upon the conscience, is exceeding terrible and dreadful. *Mine iniquity* (so the Hebrew) *is greater than I can bear*; sin or iniquity is often put for the punishment of sin, by a Metonimy of the efficient for the effect; for sin is the natural parent of punishment. *Mine iniquity* saith *Cain*, *is so great, and lyes so heavy, so terrible and dreadful upon my conscience, that it cannot bee forgiven*; and thus by his diffidence hee stabs two at once, the mercy of God, and his own soul. So *Judas, I have sinned, in that I have betrayed innocent blood, and hee went and hanged himself.*

As there is no fighting with a mighty fire, so there is no bearing up, when God sets home sin upon the conscience; a man will then chuse strangling, or hanging, rather than living under such wounds and lashes of conscience.

Histories

Gen. 4. 13
Mentiris Cain, thou liest *Cain*, saith one on the Text.

Mat. 27. 3, 4, 5.

Histories abound with instances of this nature; but I must hasten to a close.

Secondly, Fire is most dangerous and pernicious when it breaks forth of the chimny, or of the house, so it is with sin. Sin is bad in the eye, worse in the tongue, worser in the heart, but worst of all in the life. Fire when out of its proper place, may do much hurt in the house, but when it flames abroad, then it doth most mischief to others.

Sin in the heart may undo a man, but Sin in the life may undo others, as well as a mans self. Set a guard upon the eye, a greater upon thy heart, but the greatest of all upon thy life.

Salvian relates how the Heathen did reproach some Christians, who by their lewd lives, made the Gospel of Christ to bee a reproach, where (said they) is that good Law which they do beleeve? where are those rules

marginalia: 2 Sam. 12. 9, 10, 11, 12, 13, 14, 15.

Job 31. 1. Pro. 4. 23. Eph. 5. 15.

Salvianus de G.D.l.4.

of godliness which they do learn as they read the holy Gospel, and yet are unclean; they hear the Apostles writings, and yet are drunk; they follow Christ, and yet disobey Christ; they profess a holy Law, and yet do lead impure lives.

But the lives of other Christians have been so holy, that the very Heathens observing them, have said, surely this is a good God, whose servants are so good.

It is brave when the life of a Christian is a Commentary upon Christs life.

One speaking of the Scripture, saith, (*verba vivenda, non legenda*) they are words to bee lived, and practised, not read onely. *Augustin.*

A Heathen adviseth us to demean our selves so circumspectly, as if our enemies did alwaies behold us. And said another for shame, either live as Stoicks, or leave off the name of Stoicks. Sirs, live as Christians, or lay down the name of Christians. *Plutarch.*

Epictetus.

Thirdly,

Thirdly, Fire hardens, it makes the weak and limber clay to become stiff and strong for the Potters use. So sin hardens, it hardens the heart against the commands of God, the calls of Christ, and the wrestlings of the spirit.

Jer. 5. 3. ch. 19. ult. Isa. 9. 13.

As you see in *Pharaoh*, the *Jews*, and most that are under the sound of the Gospel.

Jer. 2. 25. ch. 18. 12.

Ah! how many hath this fire (sin) hardened in these daies, by working them to slight soul-softening means, and by drawing them to entertain hardening-thoughts of God, and to fall in with soul-hardening company, and soul-hardening principles, and soul-hardening examples, of hardened and unsensible Sinners? one long since thus complained, that they did (*patientius ferre Christi jacturam, quam suam*) more calmly pass by the injuries done to Christ, than those which are done unto themselves; This age is full of such hardened unsensible souls.

Fourthly,

Fourthly, Fire is a lively active element, so is sin.

Ah! how lively and active was this fire in *Abraham, David, Job, Peter, Paul,* and other Saints? though Christ by his death hath given it its mortal wound, yet it lives, and is, and will bee active in the dearest Saints. Though sin and grace were not born together, neither shall they dye together; yet while beleevers live in this world, they must live together. There is a History that speaks of a Fig-tree that grew in a stone wall, and all means was used to kill it, they cut off the branches, and it grew again, they cut down the body, and it grew again, they cut it up by the root, and still it lived, and grew until they pulled down the stone-wall; till death shall pull down our stone-walls, sin will live, this fire will burn.

Wee may say of sin, as some say of Cats, that they have many lives; kill them and they will live

Gen. 22.
Psal. 51.
Job 3.
Mat. 26.
Rom. 1.
15, &c.

Isodore the Monk, was very much out, who vaunted that he had felt in himself no motion to sin forty years together.

live again, kill them again, and they will live again; so kill sin once, and it will live again, kill it again, and it will live again, &c. Sin oftentimes is like that Monster *Hydra*, cut off one head, and many will rise up in its room.

Fifthly: Fire is of a penetrating nature, it peirceth and windeth it self into every corner and chink, and so doth sin winde it self into our thoughts, words, and works; it will winde it self into our understandings, to darken them; and into our judgements, to pervert them; and into our wills, to poison them; and into our affections, to disorder them; and into our consciences, to corrupt them; and into our carriages, to debase them. Sin will winde it self into every duty, and every mercy, it will winde it self into every one of our enjoyments and concernments.

Hannibal having overcome the *Romans*, put on their armour on

---

Isa. 1. 5, 6
Rom. 7. 13, 17
Sinne is (*malum Catholicum*) A Catholick evil.
(*Quodcunque in peccato, peccatum est*) whatsoever is in sin, is sin.

on his Souldiers; and so by that policy, they being taken for *Romans*, won a City; but what are *Hannibals* wiles, to sins wiles, or Satans wiles? if you have a minde to bee acquainted with their wiles, look over my Treatise, called, *Precious Remedies against Satans Devices.*

    Sixthly and Lastly, Fire is a devouring, a consuming element, it turns all fuel into ashes; It is a Wolf that eats up all; so sin is a fire that devours and consumes all, it turned *Sodom* and *Gomorrah* into ashes, it hath destroyed the *Chaldean*, *Persian*, and *Grecian* Kingdomes, and will at last destroy the *Roman* Kingdome also; this Woolf ate up *Sampsons* strength, *Absoloms* beauty, *Achitophels* policy, and *Herods* glory, &c. It hath drowned one world already, and will at last burn another, even this. Oh the hopes, the hearts, the happinesse, the joyes, the comforts, the souls that this fire (sin) hath con-

Psa. 21. 9

2 Pet. 2. 5, 6
Prov. 6. 32
Eccl. 9. 18
Pro. 13. 13
ch. 20. 29,
1
Pro. 11.
3. ch. 15.
25. ch. 21.
7

consumed and destroyed! &c.

Peter Camois a Bishop of *Berry* in *France*, in his draught of Eternity, *Numb.* 7.5. tells us, that some devout personages caused those words of the Prophet *Isaiah* (to bee written in Letters of Gold upon their Chimney-peeces) *who among us shall dwell with the devouring fire? who among us shall dwell with everlasting burnings?*

Isa. 33.14

Ah! young men, young men, I desire that you may alwaies look upon sin under the notion of fire, yea, as such fire as laies the foundation for everlasting fire, for everlasting burnings, and this may work when other things will not.

I have read of a grave and chaste Matron, who being moved to commit folly with a lewd Ruffian, after some discourse, shee called for a pan of burning coals, requesting him for her sake to hold his finger in them but one hour, hee answered, it is

an

an unkind request, to whom shee replied, that seeing hee would not do so much as to put one finger upon the coals for one hour, shee could not yeeld to do that, for which shee should bee tormented, both body and soul in Hell fire for ever. The Application is easie, &c.

4 Notion.

Fourthly, *If you would break with sin betimes, if you would arm against sin in the spring and morning of your daies, then you should look upon sin under the notion of a Theef.*

And indeed sin is the greatest Theef, the greatest Robber in the world; it robbed the Angels of all their glory, it robbed *Adam* of his Paradise and felicity, and it hath robbed all the sons of *Adam* of five precious Jewels, the least of which was more worth than Heaven and Earth.

2 Pet. 2. 4
Gen. 3.

1 It hath robbed them of the holy and glorious Image of God, which would have been fairly engraven

graven upon them, had *Adam* stood, &c.

2 It hath robbed them of their Son-ship, and of sons have made them slaves.

3 It hath robbed them of their friendship, and made them enemies.

4 It hath robbed them of their communion and fellowship with Father, Son, and Spirit, and made them strangers and Aliens.

5 It hath robbed them of their glory, and made them vile and miserable. It hath robbed many a Nation of the Gospel, and many a Parish of many a happy guide, and many a Christian of the favour of God, the joyes of the Spirit, and the Peace of Conscience.

Oh! the health, the wealth, the honour, the friends, the relations that sin hath robbed thousands of.

Nay, It hath robbed many of their gifts, their arts, their parts, their memory, their judgement, yea,

[margin:] Well did one of the Fathers call Pride and Vain-glory, the sweet spoiler of spiritual excellencies, and a pleasant Theef.

Young Men.

yea, their very reason, as you may see in *Pharaoh*, *Nebuchadnezzar*, *Belshazzar*, *Achitophel*, *Haman*, *Herod*, and those *Babylonish* Princes that accused *Daniel*.

And so in *Menippus* of *Phenicia*, who having lost his goods, strangled himself. And so *Dinarcus Phidon*, at a certain loss, cut his own throat to save the charge of a Cord. And so *Augustus Cæsar* (in whose time Christ was born) was so troubled and astonished at the relation of an overthrow from *Varus*, that for certain months together, hee let the hair of his head and beard grow still, and wore it long; yea, and other whiles would run his head against the doors, crying out, *Quintilius Varus*, deliver up my Legions again; by all which it is most apparent, that sin is the greatest theef in all the world. *[Suetonius.]*

Oh! Then who would not break league and Covenant with it, and bee still in pressing of God to do Justice upon it? &c.

Fifthly,

5 Notion.

Fifthly, *If you would break with sin, and arm and fence your selves against sin betimes, then you must look upon sin under the notion of a burden betimes.*

And indeed, sin of all burdens is the heaviest burden in all the world. *Innumerable evils have compassed mee about, mine iniquities have taken hold upon mee, so that I am not able to look up; they are more than the hairs of my head, therefore my heart faileth mee.* And again, *Mine iniquities are gone over my head* (saith the same person) *as an heavy burden, they are too heavy for mee to bear.* Sin is a weight that easily besets poor souls, it is a burden that so troubles them, and puzzles them, that so curbs them, and girds them, that so presses, and oppresses them, as that it wrings many bitter tears from their eyes, and many sad and grievous sighs and groans from their hearts.

Again, As Sin is a burden to Christi-

Margin references: Nah. 1. 1; Hab. 1. 1; Mal. 1. 1; Psa. 40. 12; Psa. 38. 4; Heb. 12. 1; Rom. 7. 13 ult.

Chriſtians; ſo it is a burden to Heaven, it made Heaven weary to bear the Angels that fell; no ſooner had they ſinned, but Heaven groans to bee eaſed of them; and it never left groaning till juſtice had turned them a groaning to Hell. *Jude 6.*

Again, As ſin is a burden to Heaven, ſo it is a burden to the Earth, witneſs her ſwallowing up *Korah, Dathan,* and *Abiram,* their wives, children, goods, ſervants, &c. Ah ſinners! your ſins makes the very earth to groan; they make the earth weary of bearing you. Oh! how doth the earth groan and long to ſwallow up thoſe earthly wretches, whoſe hopes, whoſe hearts, are buried in the Earth, theſe ſhall have little of Heaven, but enough of Earth when they come to dye. *Numb. 16. 26. 35.*

Cornelius a Lapide, tells a ſtory, that hee heard of a famous Preacher, who ſhewing the bondage of the Creature, brings in the *Rom. 8. 19, 20, 21, 22, 23.*

Creature complaineth thus; Oh! that wee could serve such as are godly, Oh! that our substance and our flesh might bee incorporated into godly people, that so wee might rise into glory with them; Oh! that our flesh might not bee incorporated into the flesh of sinners, for if it bee, wee shall go to Hell, and would any creatures go to Hell? Oh! wee are weary of bearing sinners, wee are weary of serving of sinners; thus the creatures groan, thus the creatures complain, the sinners sins forcing them to it, &c.

Again, Sin is a burden to God, *Behold, I am pressed under you, as a Cart is pressed that is full of sheaves,* by this plain pithy countrey comparison, God shews how sadly hee is pressed and oppressed, how sorely hee is wearied and tired with those peoples sins; Divine Patience is even worn out; Justice hath lift up her hand, and will bear with them no longer. God seems to groan

Amos 2. 13.

groan under the pressure of their sinnes, as a Cart seems to do under a heavy load; of this God complains by the Prophet *Isaiah*, *Thou hast made mee to serve with thy sinnes, thou hast wearied mee with thine iniquities.* I am as weary of your sinnes, as a Travelling woman is weary of her pains, saith God. Sin was such a burden to God, that hee sweeps it off with a sweeping flood, *Gen.* 7, &c.

Isa. 43. 24

Again, Sinne is a burden to Christ, it made him sweat, as never man sweat; It made him sweat great drops of clotted or congealed blood; Sin put Christs whole body into a bloody sweat, it made him groan pittiously, when hee bare our sins in his body on the Tree. Sin made his soul heavy even to the death, and had hee not been one that was mighty, yea, that was Almighty, hee had fainted and failed under his burden. And thus you see what a burden sinne is to man, to

Luk. 22. 44. A strange watering of a Garden. *Bern.* 1 Pet. 2. 24

Isa. 9. 6.

V 4 the

the Creatures, to heaven, to earth, to God, to Christ; and therefore as you would break with sin betimes, look alwaies upon it as a burden, yea, as the greatest and heaviest burden in all the world, &c.

6 Notion.

Sixthly and lastly, *If you would break Covenant with sin, and arm, and fence your selves against it betimes, then you must look upon it betimes under the notion of a Tyrant.*

Tit. 3. 3.

And indeed, sin is the worst and greatest Tyrant in the world. Other Tyrants can but tyrannize over our bodies, but sin is a Tyrant that tyrannizes over both body and soul, as you may see in the sixth and seventh of the *Romans*; sin is a Tyrant that hath a kind of jurisdiction in most mens hearts, it sets up the Law of Pride, the Law of Passion, the Law of Oppression, the Law of Formality, the Law of Hypocrisie, the Law of Carnality, the Law of Self-love, the

the Law of Carnal Reason, the Law of Unbeleef, and strictly commands subjection to them, and proclaims fire and sword to all that stand out; this Saints and sinners, good men and bad, do sufficiently experience.

Sin is a Tyrant of many thousand years standing, and though it hath had many a wound, and many a foil, and received much opposition, yet still it plaies the Tyrant all the world over. O! the hearts that this Tyrant makes to ake, the souls that this Tyrant makes to bleed.

Pharaohs tyranny was nothing to sins tyranny, this Tyrant will not so much as suffer his slaves to sleep. They sleep not, except they have done mischief, and their sleep is taken away, unless they cause some to fall. The wicked are like the troubled Sea, when it cannot rest, whose waters cast up mire and dirt. *There is no peace to the wicked, saith my God.*

Other Tyrants have been brought

Thales, one of the seven Sages, used to say, that few Tyrants lived to be old, but it is far otherwise with this Tyrant Sin.

Pro. 4. 16

Isa. 57. 20, 21.

brought down, and brought under by a humane power, but this cannot, but by a divine, the power of man hath brought down many of the Tyrants of this world, but it is onely the power of Christ, that can bring down this Tyrant, that can cast down his strong holds, 2 Cor. 10. 3, 4, 5, 6, &c. therefore engage Christ in the conflict, draw him into the battel, and in the end the conquest will bee yours.

Vitellius, who had been Emperor of all the world, yet was driven thorow the streets of *Rome* stark naked, and thrown into the River *Tyber*, &c.

Andronicus the Emperour, for his cruelty towards his people, was by them at last shamefully deposed, and after many contumelies, hanged up by his heels.

Ptolomy was put on a Cross. *Bajazet* in an Iron Cage. *Phocas* broken on the wheel. *Lycaon* cast to the Doggs (as well as *Jezabel*.) *Attalus* thrust into a Forge. King *Gath* into a beer-barrel, &c. But none of of these that have tamed these tyrants, that have brought down these mighty *Nimrods*, have been able to tame, to bring under the Tyrants, the sins, the lusts, that have been in their own bosomes; many a man hath had a hand in bringing down of worldly Tyrants, who notwithstanding have died for ever by the hand of a Tyrant within, &c.

CHAP. VIII.

ANd thus much for the Directions that young men must follow, if they would bee good betimes, if they would seek and serve the Lord in the spring and morning of their daies. I shall now give some brief answers to the Young mans Objections, and the Old mans scruples, and so close up this discourse.

Object. 1.

But some young men may object and say, You would have us to bee good betimes, and to seek and serve the
Lord

Lord in the Prime-rose of our daies, But it may bee time enough hereafter to follow this Counsel; wee are young, and it may bee time enough for us to minde these things hereafter, when wee have satisfied the flesh so and so, or when wee have got enough of the world, and laid up something that will stand us in stead, and that may oyl our joynts when wee are old. Now

To this Objection I answer,

First, That it is the greatest folly and madness in the world to put off God, and the great things of eternity, with may-bees; what Trades-man, what Merchant, what Mariner, so mad, so foolish, so blockish, as to put off a present season, a present opportunity of profit and advantage, upon the account of a may-bee? It may be I may have as good a season, it may bee I shall have as golden an opportunity to get, and to inrich my self as this is; and therefore farewel to this. No men that are in their right minds will argue

Objections Answered. 301

argue thus; and why then should you, especially in the things that are of an everlasting concernment to you?

I have read of one *Monarcho*, a frantick *Italian*, who thought that all the Kings of the Earth were his Vassals, and as frantick are they, who wilfully neglect present seasons of grace, upon the account of a future may-bee, &c.

Secondly, I answer, it may be if thou neglectest this present season and opportunity of grace, thou mayest never have another; it may be mercy may never knock more, if thou dost not now open; it may be Christ shall never be offered to thee more, if now thou dost not close with him, and accept of him; it may be the Spirit will never strive more with thee, if now thou dost resist him, and withstand him; it may bee a pardon shall never bee offered to thee more, if now thou wilt not take it; it may bee the Gospel shall never sound more in thy ears, if
now

Young men, if you will but go into burial places, you shall finde graves exactly of your length.

now thou wilt not hear it, now set one may-be against another may-be, set Gods may-be against thine own may-be; but,

Thirdly, Doubtless there are many thousand thousands now in Hell, who have pleased themselves, and put off God, and the seasons of grace, with a may-bee, hereafter may bee time enough. It may bee when I have gratified such a lust, and when I have treasured so much of the world, I will return, and seek, and serve the Lord, but before ever this season or opportunity came, justice hath cut the threed of their lives, and they are now miserable for ever; and now they are still a cursing themselves, because they have slipt their golden opportunities upon the account of a may-be, &c. But

Fourthly and lastly, This putting off of God, and the present seasons of Grace with a may-bee, is very provoking to God, as you may see, if you will but read, from

It was an unspeakable vexation to King Lysimachus, that his staying to drink one draught of water lost him his Kingdome

from the 20. verse to the 33. of the first of *Proverbs*. Nothing stirs and provokes a Master more, than his servants putting off his service or his commands with a may-bee; it may be I will, it may bee I may do this and that; nothing puts a Master sooner into a heat, a flame, than this; nor nothing puts God more into a flame than this, as you may see by comparing, *Psal.* 95. *vers.* 6. to the end, with that 3 of the *Hebrews*, and the 7, 8, 9, 10, 11, 15, 16, 17, 18, 19. read the words, and tremble at the thought of a may-bee, at the thoughts of putting off of God, and the seasons of Grace.

I have read of two, who cut off their right hand one for another, and then made it an excuse, a put off, they were lame, and so could not serve in the Gallies of *Francis* the first, King of *France*, but this practice of theirs did so insense and provoke the King, that hee sent them both to the Gallows.

I suppose the Reader is not so young, but knows how to apply it.

Object. 2.

If I should begin to bee good betimes, and to seek and serve the Lord in the spring and morning of my daies, I should lose my friends, I should lose their favour, for they are carnal and worldly, and had rather I should seek after gold, than God, the Creature, than Christ, Earth, than Heaven, &c.

Now to this I answer, Surely you are out, for

First, This is the high-way, the ready way to gain the best, the surest, and the soundest friends. *When a mans waies please the Lord, hee maketh even his enemies to bee at peace with him.* When a man falls in with God, God will work the Creatures to fall in with him. *Joseph* found it so, and *Jacob* found it so, and *Job* found it so, the three children

Pro. 16. 7

Job 5, 23, -- 28.

found

found it so, and *Daniel* found it so, as you all know that have but read the Scripture. And many in this age (as bad as it is) have found, that the best way to make friends, is first, to make God our friend. Ah! young men, young men, you shall not lose your friends (by seeking and serving of the Lord in the spring and morning of your daies) but onely exchange bad ones for good ones, the worst for the best; hee that gives up himself betimes to the Lord, shall have God for his friend, and Christ for his friend, and the Angels for his friends, and the Saints for his friends; Christ will bee to such,

First, *An omnipotent friend.* Secondly, *An omniscient friend.* Thirdly, *An omnipresent friend.* Fourthly, *An indeficient friend.* Fifthly, *An independent friend.* Sixthly, *An immutable friend.* Seventhly, *A watchful friend.* Eightly, *A loving friend.* Ninthly, *A faithful friend.* Tenthly, *A compassionate friend.* Eleventhly, *A close friend.*

Luk.15.7. 10.
Isa.6.7,8,9.
Heb.4.13.
Isa.59.16,17
Isa.44.24
Mal.3.6
Psal.121.4,5

X   There

There is a friend that sticketh closer than a Brother, Prov. 18, 24. such a friend is Christ, and such a friend is as ones own soul, a rare happinesse, hardly to bee match'd.

Twelfthly, *An universal friend, a friend in all cases, and a friend in all places.* Christ is so a friend to every one of his, as if hee were a friend to none besides: Hence it is that they say, not onely our Lord, our God, but my Lord, and my God. Christ is such an universal friend, as that hee supplies the place, and acts the part of every friend.

Thirteenthly, *Hee is our first friend*, Psal. 90. 1. before wee had a friend in all the world, hee was our friend, Prov. 8. 21.

Lastly, *Hee is a constant friend, Whom hee loves, hee loves to the end.*

Augustus Cæsar would not suddenly entertain a league of friendship with any, but was a constant friend to those hee loved

---

1 John 4. 16.
Tit. 1. 2.
Isa. 63. 9

Luk. 1. 43
Joh. 20. 28
Phil. 4. 19

Joh. 13. 1.
Alexander the Great, cannot but that knot of friendship that is tied betwixt Christ and his

Objections Answered

ed (*Amare nec cito desisto, nec temere incipio*) late ere I love, as long ere I leave; Where Christ begins to love, hee alwaies loves, *Jer. 31.3. I have loved thee with an everlasting love*: Now who would not venture the loss of all friends in the world, to gain such a friend as this is?

Ah! Young men and women, let mee say to you, what *Seneca* said to his friend *Polibius*, (*Fas tibi non est de fortuna conqueri, salvo Cæsare*) never complain of thy hard fortune, as long as *Cæsar* is thy friend; so say I, never complain of your losse of Friends, so long as by losing of them, you gain Christ to be your Friend.

Secondly, Thou were't better bee without their friendship and favour, than to injoy it upon any sinful and unworthy accounts, thou were't better run the hazard of losing thy friends, and their favour, by seeking and serving the Lord in the Prime-

X 2 rose

rose of thy daies, than to run the hazard of losing God, Christ, Heaven, Eternity, and thy Soul for ever, by neglecting the things of thy peace.

Mat. 10. 26.
Mar. 8. 36

It was a gallant return which the noble *Rutilius* made his friend, requesting of him an unlawful favour, in such language as this, I had as good bee without such a friend, as with him who will not let mee speed in what I ask; to whom hee replied, I can want such a friend as you, if for your sake, I must do that which is not honest.

The Application is easie.

Well Young men, remember this, the torments of a thousand hells, were there so many, comes far short of this one voice, to bee turned out of Gods presence with a (*Non novi vos*) I know you not.

Mat. 7.23

Ah! Young man, Young man, thou were't better ten thousand thousand times to bee cast out of the thoughts and

hearts

Objections Answered.

hearts of thy carnal friends, and relations, than to bee cast out of Gods presence with cursed *Cain*, for ever, than to bee excommunicated out of the general Assembly of the Saints, and Congregation of the first-born which are written in Heaven; and therefore away with this Objection; But,

Thirdly, The favour and friendship of such carnal persons, is very fickle and inconstant, it is very fading and withering; Now they stroake, and anon they strike; now they lift up, and anon they cast down; now they smile, and anon they frown; now they kiss, and anon they kill; now they cry *Hosanna, Hosanna*, and anon they cry, crucifie him, crucifie him; *Haman* is one day feasted with the King, and the next day made a feast for Crows; The Princes of *Babylon* were highly in King *Darius* his favour one day, and cast into the Lions den the next; The Scribes and Pharises that

Gen. 4.

Heb. 12; 23

Esth. 7.

Dan. 6.

cry-

cried up *Judas* one day, did in effect bid him go and hang himself the next day.

Such mens favour and friendship, are as *Venice* glasses, quickly broken; and therefore not much to bee prized or minded. Histories abound with instances of this nature; but I must hasten, onely remember this, that every daies experience tells us, that wicked men can soon turn Tables, and cross their books, their favour and friendship is usually like to a morning cloud, or like to *Jonas* Gourd, one hour flourishing, and the next hour withering, and why then shouldest thou set thy heart upon that which is more changeable than the Moon? But

Fourthly and lastly, Who but a mad man would adventure the loss of the Kings favour to gain the favour of his Page? who but a stark *Bedlam* would run the hazard of losing the Judges favour upon the Bench, to purchase

Marginalia:
Mat. 27. 3, 4. *Valerian, Valens, Bellisarius, Bajazet, Pythias, Dionysius, Pompey, William* the Conqueror and many others have found it so.

Glaucus, who changed his armour of gold with *Diomedes* for his armour of Brasse, stands upon record for a fool.

chase the good will of the prisoner at the bar?

Socrates preferred the Kings countenance before his Coin; and so must you prefer the favour of God, the countenance of Christ, and the things of eternity, above all the favour and friendship of all the men in the world; when your nearest friends and dearest relations stands in competition with Christ, or the things above, you must shake them off, you must turn your backs upon them, and welcome Christ, and the things of your peace; hee that forsakes all relations for Christ, shall certainly finde all relations in Christ, he will be father, friend, husband, childe; hee will bee every thing to thee, who takest him for thy great all.

Psa. 4. 6, 7

Psa. 45. 10
Matth. 10. 37
Luke 14. 26, 27.

Object. 3.

I but I shall meet with many reproaches from one and other, if I should labour to bee good betimes; If I should seek and serve the Lord in the spring and morning of my youth.

Now to this I answer,

First, What are Reproaches to the great things that others have suffered, for Christ, his Gospel, and the maintaining of a good Conscience? what is a prick of a pin, to a stab at the heart? what is a chiding, to a hanging, a whipping, to a burning? no more are all the reproaches thou canst meet with, to the great things that others have suffered for Christs sake.

Hebrews ch. 10, 11. read the ten persecutions.

Ah! Young men, you should bee like the *Scythian* that went naked in the Snow, and when *Alexander* wondred how hee could endure it, answered, I am not ashamed, for I am all forehead.

So should you in the cause and way of Christ, you should not bee ashamed, you should bee all forehead, you should be stout and bold.

Colonus the *Dutch* Martyr, under all his reproaches, called to the Judge that had sentenced him to death, and desired him to lay his hand

Objections Answered.

hand upon his heart, and then asked him, whose heart did most beat, his or the Judges; All the reproaches in the world, should not so much as make a Christians heart beat, they should not in the least trouble him, nor disturb him; But,

Secondly, I answer, That all the reproaches thou meetest with in the way of Christ, and for the sake of Christ, they do but adde Pearls to thy Crown, they are all additions to thy happinesse and blessednesse. If yee bee reproached for the name of Christ, happy are yee; for the Spirit of Glory, and of God, resteth upon you; on their part, hee is evil spoken of, but on your part hee is glorified; the more you are reproached for Christs sake on earth, the greater shall bee your reward in Heaven, they that are most loaded with Reproaches here, shall bee most laden with glory hereafter. Christ hath written their Names in golden Letters in his book,

1 Pet. 4. 14

Mat. 5. 11, 12.

The Young Mans

book of Life, that are written in black Letters of reproach for his sake on Earth. 'Twas a good saying of one, a Reproacher (saith hee) is beneath a man, but the Reproached that bear it well, are equal to Angels; of all Crowns, the reproached mans Crown, will weigh heaviest in Heaven. But,

Thirdly, A answer, the best men have been mostly reproached, *David* was, *Psalm* 69. 7. *Psalm* 89. 50. *Psal.* 119. 22. *Psalm* 31. 11. *Psal.* 109. 25. and *Job* was, *Job* 19. 35. ch. 20. 3. *Job* 16. 10. and *Jeremiah* was, *Jer.* 20. 7, 10. Yea, this hath been the common portion of the people of God in all ages of the World, in *Nehemiah's* time it was so, *Neh.* 1. 3. *And they said unto mee, the remnant that are left of the captivity, are in great affliction and reproach.* In *Davids* time it was so, *Psalm* 79. 4. and *Psalm* 44. 13, 14. And in *Jeremiah's* time it was so, *Lam.* 5. 1. *Remember, O Lor,*

Chrysost. So was *Joseph, Mephibosheth, Naboth*, and in latter times, *Luther*, whom they said died despairing when hee was alive to confute it. And that *Beza* run away with another mans wife. And that *Calvin* was branded on the shoulder for a rogue but there would bee no end of this stuff, should I say all that might bee said.

Lord, what is come upon us, consider and behold our reproach. And in *Daniel*'s time it was so, *Dan.* 9. 16. *Thy people are become a reproach to all that are about us*, and it was so in the Apostles time, *Rom.* 3. 8. *And not rather as wee be slanderously reported*, as some affirm that wee say, *let us do evil, that good may come, whose damnation is just*, 2 *Cor.* 6. 8. *By honour, and dishonour; by evil report, and good report; as Deceivers, and yet true:* so in that, 1 *Tim.* 4. 10. *For therefore wee both labour and suffer reproach, because wee trust in the living God,* &c. And it was so in the Primitive times, for when the Christians met together before Sun to pray, the Heathens reported of them, that they worshiped the Sun, and aspired after Monarchy, and committed Adulteries, and unnatural uncleannesses: Now who is troubled, who complains of that which is a common lot, as cold, win-

Tertullian.

Winter, Sicknesse, Death, &c. No more should any complain of reproaches, it being the common lot of the people of God in all ages; yea, Christ himself was sadly reproached, falsly accused, and strangely traduced, disgraced, and scandalized; hee was called a Glutton, a Drunkard, a friend of Publicans and Sinners, and judged to use the black Art, casting out Devils by *Beelzebub* the Prince of Devils; Christ hath suffered the greatest, and the worst Reproaches, why then should you be afraid to wear that Crown of Thorns that Christ hath wore before you? there is a great truth in what hee said, (*Non potest qui pati timet, ejus esse qui passus est*) hee that is afraid to suffer, cannot bee his Disciple, who suffered so much; if the Master hath been marked with a black coal, let not the servant think to go free. I am heartily angry (saith *Luther*) with those that speak of my sufferings, which

Mat. 9.34. ch. 12. 24

Tertul. de fuga in persecut.

Objections Answered. 317

which if compared with that which Christ suffered for mee, are not once to bee mentioned in the same day; But,

Fourthly, I answer, that all reproachers shall at last bee arraigned at the highest bar of justice, for all the reproaches that they have cast upon the people of God.

They think it strange (or they think it a new world) that you run not with them to the same excess of riot, speaking evil of you: who shall give account to him that is ready to judge the quick and the dead.

1 Pet. 4. 4 Xenizontai Blasphemountes. Wonder and Blasphem.

I am in an extasie (saith *Picus Mirandula*) to think how prophane men rail upon those now, whom one day they will wish they had imitated. It was excellent counsel that the Heathen Oratour gave his hearers (*ita vivamus, ut rationem nobis reddendam arbitremur*) let us live as those that must give an account of all at last.

Cic. 4. in Verr.

Chrysostome brings in Christ com-

comforting his Disciples against reproaches, speaking thus unto them; what is the wrong grievous to you? that now they call you Seducers, and Conjurers, it will not bee long before they shall openly call you the Saviours and blessings of the whole World, that time that shall declare all things that are now hid, shall rebuke them for their lying words against you, and shall kindle the splendor of your virtue; So they shall be found Lyers, evil speakers, false accusers of others; but you shall bee more clear and illustrious than the Sun, and you shall have all men witnesses of your glory. Such as wisely and humbly bear reproaches now, shall judge reproachers at last. But,

Fifthly, I answer, That God doth many times, even in this life; bear sad witness and testimony against the reproachers of his people; *I will bless them that bless thee, and I will curse them that*

Mal. 3. 19
Mic. 7. 9, 10, 11
1 Cor. 6. 3, 4

Gen. 12.3
2 Sam.16. 11, 12, 13

Objections Answered.

that curse thee; God will even in this life curse them with a witness, who curse them that hee blesseth; *Pharaoh* found it so, and *Saul* found it so, and *Jezabel* found it so, and *Haman* found it so, and the Princes of *Babylon* found it so, and the *Jews* find it so to this very day.

And Oh the dreadful judgements and curses that God hath poured out upon the reproachers of his Name, of his Son, of his Spirit, of his Word, of his Ordinances, and of his people, in these daies wherein wee live. I might give you many sad instances of such in our daies, whose feet justice hath taken in the snare, men of abstracted conceits, and sublime speculations, and indeed such usually prove the great wise fools, who like the Lark, soareth higher and higher, peering, and peering, till at length they fall into the net of the fowler, and no wonder, for such persons usually are as censorious,

Divine justice is like Vulcans Iron net, that took the Gods, it apprehends and condemns all that are reproachers, and enemies to his people.

as they are curious.

Sixthly, I answer, *Paul* rejoyced more in his suffering Reproaches for Christs sake, than hee did in his being wrapt up in the third Heaven, 2 *Cor.* 12. 10. *Therefore I take pleasure in infirmities, in reproaches, in necessities, in persecutions, in distresses, for Christs sake, for when I am weak, then am I strong.* And therefore you have him often a singing this song, *I Paul a Prisoner of Jesus Christ*: not I *Paul* wrapt up in the third Heaven: Hee look't upon all his sufferings, as Gods love-tokens, hee look't upon all reproaches, as pledges and badges of his Son-ship; and therefore joyes and glories under all. Christ shewed his love to him in wraping him up in the third Heaven, and hee shewed his love to Christ, in his joyful bearing of Reproaches for his sake. *Paul* rattles his chain (which hee bears for the Gospel) and was proud of it, as a Woman of her Ornaments, saith *Chrysostome*. Now

(*Crudelitas vestra gloria nostra*) your cruelty, is our glory, said they in *Tertullian*; fire, sword, prison, famine, are all delightfull to mee saith *Basil*.

Objections Answered.

Now why should that bee matter of trouble and discouragement to you, that was matter of joy and rejoycing to him? shall hee look upon Reproaches as a Crown of honour, and will you look upon Reproaches as a Crown of thorns?

O! look upon Reproach as a Royal Diadem, look upon it as Christs Livery, and count it your highest ambition in this world, to wear this Livery for his sake, who once wore a Crown of Thorns for your sakes; When *Babylas* was to dye, hee required this favour, to have his chains buried with him as the ensigns of his honour. But

Seventhly, I answer, That by a wise and gracious behaviour under the Reproaches thou meetest with for Christs sake, thou mayest bee instrumental to win others to Christ.

It was a notable saying of *Luther* (*ecclesia totum mundum convertit sanguine & oratione*) the Church con-

Sufferings are the ensigns of heavenly Nobility, saith Calvin.

It was an observation of Mr. John Lindsay, that the very smoak of Mr. Hamilton, converted as many as it blew upon.

converted the whole world by blood and prayer.

Divers have been won to Christ, by beholding the gracious carriages of Christians under their sufferings and reproaches for Christ.

Wee read of *Cicilia*, a poor virgin, who by her gracious behaviour under all her sufferings and reproaches for Christ, was the means of converting four hundred to Christ.

Adrianus beholding the gracious chearful carriages of the Martyrs, under all their sufferings and reproaches, was converted to Christ, and afterwards suffered martyrdome for Christ.

Justin Martyr was also converted, by observing the holy and chearful behaviour of the Saints, under all their sufferings and reproaches for Christ. During the cruel persecutions of the Heathen Emperours, the Christian Faith was spread thorow all places of the Empire, because the oftner

See also the History of the Council of Trent. 418. 2. Edit.

oftner they were mown down (saith *Tertullian*) the more they grew.

And *Austin* observed, that though there were many thousands put to death for professing Christ, yet they were never the fewer for being slain.

Ah! Young men, you may by a wise and gracious bearing of Reproaches for Christ, bee instrumental to win others to Christ; and therefore never plead there is a Lion in the way; but I must hasten; and therefore in the eighth and

Last place, consider, how bravely several of the very Heathens have bore reproaches, and let that provoke you, in the face of all reproaches, to seek and serve the Lord in the morning of your youth, &c.

When *Demosthenes* was reproached by one, I will not, saith hee, strive with thee in this kind of fight, in which he that is overcome is the better man.

When one came and reproached *Xenophon*, saies hee, you have learned how to reproach, and I have learned how to bear Reproach.

And *Aristippus* (the Philosopher) said, you are fit to cast reproaches, and I am fit to bear reproaches.

Demochares an Athenian Oratour, was sent to King *Philip* as Embassadour, *Philip* asked him, how hee might pleasure the *Athenians*, for-sooth, said hee, if you will hang your self; the Prince patiently sent him home again, and bid him ask whether were more Noble, the patient hearer, or venter of such unseemly language.

When one wondred at the patience of *Socrates* towards one who reviled and reproached him; if wee should meet one, saith hee, whose body were more unsound than ours, should wee bee angry with him, and not rather pitty him? why then should wee not

Objections Answered.

not do the like to him whose soul is more diseased than ours?

Augustus Cæsar, (in whose time Christ was born) bid *Catullus* the railing Poet to Supper, to shew that hee had forgiven him.

It is a notable Example that wee finde of one *Pericles*, who as hee was sitting with others in a great meeting, a foul-mouthed fellow bitterly reproached him, and railed all the day long upon him, and at night when it was dark, and the meeting up, the Fellow followed him, and railed at him, even to his door, and hee took no notice of him, but when hee came at home, this is all hee said, friend it is dark, I pray let my man light you home.

Josephus reports of that *Herod* that is made mention of in *Act.* 12. 23. that when one *Simon* a Lawyer, had grievously reproached and scandalized him before the people, hee sent for him

Plutarch in vita Peric.

Themistocles professed, that if two waies were shewed him, one to Hell, and the other to the bar, hee would chuse that which went to Hell, and forsake the other.

him, and caused him to sit down next to him, and in a kind manner hee spake thus to him. Tell mee, I pray thee, what thing thou seest fault-worthy, or contrary to the Law, in mee? *Simon* not having any thing to answer, besought him to pardon him, which the King did, and was friends with him, and dismissed him, bestowing gifts on him.

Ah! Young men, young men, shall the very Heathen make nothing of Reproaches, shall they bear up so prudently and bravely under the greatest loads of reproaches, and will not you? will not you, who in your light, in your mercies, and in all Gospel engagements, are so highly advanced above them? Oh that none of them may bee called to the Bar in the great day, to witness against any of you, into whose hands this Treatise shall fall; and so much by way of Answer to the third Objection. But,

4 Object.

4 Object.

Fourthly, The young man objects and saies, *you press us to bee good betimes, and to seek and serve the Lord in the spring and morning of our daies, but wee observe, that most men minde not these things, but rather give liberty to themselves, to walk in waies that are most pleasing to the flesh, and why then should wee be singular and nice, wee were better do as the most do? &c.* Now to this I answer.

1 That though bad examples are dangerous to all, yet usually they prove most dangerous and pernicious to young persons, who are more easily drawn to follow examples, than precepts, especially those examples that tend most to undo them, 2 *King.* 15. 9. It is said of *Zachariah*, the King of *Israel*, that hee did evil in the sight of the Lord, *as his Fathers had done*, hee departed *not from the sins of Jeroboam*, hee would bee as his Father was, and do as his Father did, what ever came on it.

Præcepta docent, exempla movent, Precepts may instruct, but examples do perswade.

So the *Samaritans*, of whom it is said, 2 *King.* 17. 41. *These Nations feared the Lord* (that is, they made some kinde of profession of the true Religion, as the ten Tribes had done) *and served their graven Images* (too) *both their children, and their childrens children,* (did thus) *as did their Fathers, so do they unto this day*: By evil examples they were both drawn to Idolatry, and rooted and confirmed in it; so the main reason why the Kingdome and Church of *Judah* were so setled in their Idolatry, that there was no hope of reclaiming them, was this, that their children remembred their Altars and their Groves by the green trees upon the high Hills, *Jer.* 17. 1, 2. Tinder is not apter to take fire, nor Wax the impression of the Seal, nor Paper the Ink, than youth is to follow ill examples.

You may see in *Radbod*, King of *Phrisia*, who coming to the Font to bee baptized, asked what was be-

Objections Answered.

become of his Ancestors, answer was made, that they died in a fearful state unbaptized, hee replied, that hee would rather perish with the multitude, than go to Heaven with a few.

I remember the Heathen brings in a young man, who hearing of the adulteries and wickednesses of the gods, said, what, do they so? and shall I stick at it? no I will not. Sinful examples are very drawing, and very incouraging, many have found it so to their eternal undoing; those that have no ears to hear what you say, have many eies to see what you do. Bad Princes make bad Subjects, bad Masters make bad Servants, bad Parents make bad Children, and bad Husbands make bad Wives; it is easier for the bad to corrupt the good, than for the good to convert the bad; it is easier to run down the Hill with company, than to run up the Hill alone.

I would desire all young men often

Æthiopians lame themselves, if their King bee lame, saith Diodorus. Ælian reports that there was a Whore that did boast that she could easily get scholars away from Socrates, but Socrates could get away no scholars from her.

often to remember that saying of *Lactantius*, (*Qui malum imitatur, bonus esse non potest*) hee who imitates the bad, cannot bee good. Young men, in these professing times, stand between good and bad examples, as *Hercules* in his dream stood between Virtue and Vice. Solicited by both, chuse you must who to follow. Oh that you were all so wise, as to follow the best; as a woman that hath many Suters, is very careful to take the best; so should you. Life, Heaven, Happiness, Eternity, hangs upon it.

But before I come to the second answer, let mee leave this note or notion with those who make no conscience of undoing others by their examples, *viz.*

That a more grievous punishment is reserved for them who cause others to offend, than for them which sin by their occasion, or example.

Thus the Serpent was punished more than *Eve*, and *Eve* more than *Adam*.

So

Sin is bad in the eye, worse in the tongue, worser in the heart, but worst of all in the life, and that because it then indangers other mens souls, as well as a mans own.

So *Jezabel* felt a greater and sorer judgement than *Ahab*. To sin (saith one) hath not so much perdition in it, as to cause others to sin. Friends, you have sins enough of your own to make you for ever miserable, why should you by giving bad examples to others, make your selves far more miserable? the lowest, the darkest, the hottest place in Hell, will bee for them that have drawn others thither by their example. *Dives* knew, that if his Brethren were damned, hee should bee double damned, because hee had largely contributed to the bringing of them to Hell by his wicked example; and therefore hee desires that they might bee kept out of Hell, (not out of any love, or good will to them) but because their coming thither would have made his hell more hot, his torments more insufferable; But

Secondly, I answer, *If you sin with others, you shall suffer with others*; if you will partake of o-
ther

Mat. 23. 15

Luke 16. 28

ther mens sins, you shall also partake of other mens plagues. They that have been (like *Simeon* and *Levi*) brethren in iniquity, they shall bee brethren in misery; they that have sinned together impenitently, shall bee sent to Hell joyntly, they shall perish together eternally. If you will needs bee companions with others in their sins, you shall bee sure to bee companions with them in their sorrows. The old world sin together, and are drowned together; the *Sodomites* burning in lusts together, were burnt with fire and brimstone together. *Korah*, *Dathan*, and *Abiram*, they sin together, they murmure and provoke the Lord together, and the earth opens her mouth, and swallows them up together. *Pharaoh* and his hosts pursue *Israel* together, and they are drowned in the Sea together. *Zimri* and *Cosbi* commit folly, uncleanness together, and *Phineas* stabs them both together. The Hebrew Doctors

Marginalia:
Rev. 18. 4
Non minus ardebit, qui cum multis ardebit *August.*
Hee burns no lesse that burns with company.

Gen. 6.
Gen. 19.

Num. 16. 26,--34

Exod. 14

Numb. 25

Doctors have a very pretty parable to this purpose; A man planted an Orchard, and going from home, was careful to leave such watch-men as might both keep it from strangers, and not deceive him themselves, therefore hee appointed one blinde, but strong of his limbs, and the other seeing, but a cripple. These two in their Masters absence conspired together, and the blind took the lame on his shoulders, and so gathered the fruit; their Master returning and finding out their subtilty, punished them both together.

So will justice deal with you at last, who sin with others; therefore take heed young men of doing as others do. But

Thirdly, I answer, *You must not live by examples, but by precepts;* you are not to look so much at what others do, as at what God requires you to do, *Exod.* 23. 2. *Thou shalt not follow a multitude to do evil, neither shalt thou speak*

Obedientia non discutit Dei mandata, sed facit. Prosper.

speak in a cause to decline after many to wrest judgement, Rom. 12. 2. *fashion not your selves like unto this word*; that is, do not fashion and conform your selves to the corrupt customes and courses of wretched worldlings, who have made Gold their God, and gain their glory; the running cross to a divine command, cost the young Prophet his life (though hee did it under pretence of Revelation from God) as you may see in that sad story, 1 *King*. 13. *ch. &c.* (*Non parentum, aut majorum authoritas, sed Dei docent is imperium*) the command of God must out-weigh all authority and example of men.

Jerome.

And wee must bee as careful in the keeping of a light Commandement, as an heavy Commandement: saith a *Rabbi*, Divine commands must bee obeyed against all contrary reasonings, wranglings, and examples. *Austin* brings in some excusing their compliance with the sinful

Objections Answered.

full customes and examples of those times, in drinking healths, thus: Great personages urged it, and it was at the Kings banquet, where they judged of loyalty by luxury, and put us upon this election, drink, or dye, the not drinking of a health had been our death; hee gives this answer, that God who sees that for love to him, and his commands, thou wouldest not conform to their drunken customes, will give thee favour in their eyes, who thus threatned thee to drink.

The complaint is antient in Seneca, that commonly men live not ad rationem, but ad similitudinem. Seneca de vita beata. c. 1.

Ah! young men, you that dote so much upon examples now, will finde that a stinging, terrifying question, when put home by God, or conscience, *who hath required these things at your hands?* Isa. 1. 12. But

Fourthly, I answer, *Company and allurements to sin, will bee found no sufficient excuse for sin.*

If *Eve* lay her fault on the Serpent, and *Adam* lay his on *Eve*, God will take it off, and lay the curse

Gen. 3.

curse on both. *Sauls* provocation by his people (and by *Samuels* long stay) to offer Sacrifice would not bear him out, but for his disobedience, hee must lose both his Crown and Life. The young man in the *Proverbs*, though tempted and solicited by the Harlot, yet hath a dart struck thorow his heart; though *Jonah* did plead Gods gracious inclinations to shew mercy, and his fear of being disproved; yea, and though hee might have pleaded his fear of cruel and savage usage from the *Ninivites* (whose hearts were desperately set upon wickedness) and his despair of ever doing good upon a people so blinded, and hardened; and that they were *Gentiles*, and hee a *Jew*, and why should hee then be sent with so strange, so terrible a message, to such a people, nothing being more hateful and distasteful to a Jewish Pallate; but all these pleas and excuses will not bear off the blow; *Jonah* must

into

1 Sam. 15.
14, 15, 26
27

Prov. 7.
14, 15, 21

Objections Answered.

into the Sea for all this, yea, hee must to the bottome of Hell, as himself phrases it. It is in vain for the bird to complain, that it saw the Corn, but not the Pit-fall, or for a fish to plead, it saw the bait, but not the hook. So it will bee in vain for sinners at last, when they are taken in an infernal pit-fall, to plead company and allurements by which they have been inticed to undo their souls for ever.

Dionysius the Sicilian King, to excuse himself from the present delivery of the golden garment hee took from his God *Apollo*, answered, that such a robe as that was, could not bee at any season of the year useful to his god, for it would not keep him warm in the winter, and it was too heavy for the summer, and so put off his Idol god; but the God of spirits, the God of all flesh, will not bee put off with any excuses or pretences, when hee shall try and judge the children of men: But

Oculos quos peccatum claudit, pæna apperit. Gre. The eyes that sin shuts, affliction opens, and *Jonah* found it so.

The Young Mans

Fifthly and lastly, I answer, *That it is a very great judgement to be given up to follow evil examples:* a man given up to evil examples, is a man sadly left of God, wofully blinded by Satan, and desperately hardened in sin; it speaks a man ripe for wrath, for ruine, for hell, *Jer.* 6. 21. * *Behold, I will lay stumbling blocks before this people, and the Fathers and the Sons together shall fall upon them; the Neighbour and his friend shall perish.* Oh! it is a dreadful thing when God shall make the sinful examples of others to bee stumblingblocks to a people, at which they shall stumble and fall, and perish, for ever; good had it been for such persons, that they had never been born, as Christ once spake concerning *Judas.*

The *Rhodians* and *Lydians* enacted several Laws, that those sons which followed not their Fathers in their virtues, but followed vicious examples, should bee disinherited, and their lands given to the

---

Mat. 18. 7

* This particle Behold is sometimes a note of derision, Gen. 3. 22
2 A note of attention often, Isa. 28. 6 Mal. 1. 1 Luk. 1. 20
3 A note of admiration often.
4 A note of asseveration.
5 A note of castigation; in all these senses wee may take it here. *Varro.*

the most virtuous of that race, not admitting any impious heir whatsoever to inherit; and do you think that God will not dis-inherit all those of Heaven and happiness, who follow vicious examples? doubtless hee will, 1 *Cor.* 10. 5, -- 12.

5 Objection.

The fifth and last Objection (I shall mention) is this, *God is a God of mercy, in him are bowels of mercy, yea a Sea, an Ocean of mercy; hee loves mercy, hee delights in mercy, and hee is ready to shew mercy to poor sinners, when they are even at the last cast, when there is but a short stride between them and the grave, between them and eternity, as wee see in his extending mercy to the Theef, and in his giving a pardon into his hand, and the assurance of Paradise into his bosome, when hee was ready to bee turned off the Ladder of life; and therefore I may spend the prime-rose of my daies in following sin and the delights, profits, vanities, and contents of this world, and at last cast, I may have mercy, as well as the Theef. God is a God made up of mercy, and surely hee will not deny some crums of mercy to a poor sinner in misery,* &c.

Now to this Objection I shall give these following answers.

First, *God is as just as hee is merciful,* witness his casting the Angels out of Heaven, and *Adam* out of Paradise; witness all the threatnings, the curses, the woes that the Bible is filled with, from one end to the other; witness the hell, the horrour, the terrour and amazement that hee raises in the consciences of sinners; witness the devastations that hee hath made of the most stately flourishing Towns, Cities, Countries and Kingdomes, that have been in all the world; witness the variety of diseases, calamities, miseries, dangers, deaths, and hells, that alwaies attend the inhabitants of the world; but above all

God is as well all-hand to punish, as hee is all grace to pardon.

Objections Answered.

all, witness Christs treading the Wine-press of his Fathers wrath; witness his hiding his face from him, and the pouring out of all his displeasure and vengeance upon him.

Zeleucus the *Locrensian* Lawgiver, thrust out one of his own Sons eyes, for his transgressing of a wholesome Law, which hee had enacted, but God the Father thrust out both Christs eies for our transgressing of his Royal Law; Oh! the justice & severity of God. But

Secondly, I answer, That there is not a greater evidence of blindness, prophaneness, hard-heartedness, spiritual madness, and hellish-desperateness in all the world, than to make that an Argument, an incouragement to sin (*viz.* the mercy of God) which should bee the greatest Argument under Heaven to keep a man from sin, as all know that have but read the Scripture, neither are there any sinners in the world, that God delights to

Valerius lib. 6. cap. 5

Z 3 rain

Read Isa. 22.12,13, 14,15. and Ezek. 24. 11,12,13, 14.

rain Hell out of Heaven upon, as upon such, who by their abuse of mercy, turn the God of mercy, into a God of clouts, and goe on out-daring justice it self, *Deut.* 29. 19, 20. *And it come to pass, when hee heareth the words of this curse, that hee bless himself in his heart, saying, I shall have peace (God is a God of mercy) though I walk in the imagination of my heart, to adde drunkenness to thirst:* The Lord will not spare him, but then the anger of the Lord, and his jealousie, shall smoak against that man, and all the curses that are written in this book, shall lye upon him, and the Lord shall blot out his name from under Heaven. In these words you may observe, that God is absolute in threatning, to shew that hee will bee resolute in punishing, *Psal.* 11. 5, 6. *The wicked, and him that loveth iniquity, doth his soul hate. Upon the wicked hee shall rain snares, fire and brimstone, and an horrible tempest; this shall be the portion of their cup.* Ah!

A lover of iniquity, is a liver in iniquity upon choice.

Objections Answere.

Ah! That all poor sinners would make these two Scriptures their companions, their constant bed-fellows, till they are got above that sad temptation of turning the mercy of God into an incouragement to sin.

Whilst *Milo Crotoniates* was tearing asunder the stock of an Oak, his strength failing him, the cleft suddenly closing, was held so fast by the hands, that hee became a prey to the beasts of the field: All the abusers of mercy, will certainly, and suddenly, become a prey to the justice of God, that will rent and tear them in peeces, as the Psalmist speaks, *Psal.* 50. 22. *Wo, wo, to that soul that fights against God with his own mercies*; that will bee bad, because hee is good; that will bee sinful, because hee is merciful; that will turn all the kindnesses of God (that should bee as so many silver cords, to tye him to love and obedience) into arrows, and so shoot them back into the

heart

heart of God. Abused mercy will at last turn into a Lion, a fierce Lion, and then wo to the abusers and despisers of it. But

Thirdly, In answer to that part of the Objection, concerning the Theef on the Crosse, I offer these things briefly to your thoughts.

First, *That as one was saved, to teach sinners not to despair, so another was damned, to teach them not to presume.*

Exemplum latronis servati est admirandum, non imitandum.

A pardon is sometimes given to one upon the Gallows, but who so trusts to that, the rope may bee his hire; It is not good (saith one) to put it upon the Psalm of *miserere*, and the neck verse; for sometimes hee proves no Clerk, and so hangs for it.

Secondly, It is an Example without a promise, here is an example of late repentance, but where is there a promise of late repentance?

Oh! Let not his late and sudden conversion, bee to thee a temp-

temptation, till thou haſt found a promiſe for late and ſudden converſion; it is not examples, but promiſes that are foundations for Faith to reſt on; hee that walks by an example of mercy, without a precept to guide him, and a promiſe to ſupport him, walks but by a dark Lanthorn, that will deceive him; well young man, remember this, examples of mercy increaſe wrath, when the heart is not bettered by them; But

Thirdly, This was a rare miracle of mercy, with the glory whereof Chriſt did honour the ignominy of his Croſs; and therefore wee may as well look for another crucifying of Chriſt, as look for a ſinners converſion, when he hath ſcarce time enough to reckon up all thoſe particular duties, which make up the integrity of its conſtitution. But

Fourthly, I anſwer, This Theef knew not Chriſt before, hee had not refuſed, neglected, nor ſlighted

slighted Christ before; the Sermon on the Cross was the first Sermon that ever hee heard Christ preach, and Christs Prayer on the Cross, was the first Prayer that ever hee heard Christ make; hee knew not Christ, till hee met him on the Cross (which proved to him a happy meeting) his case was as if a Turk, or a Heathen, should now bee converted to the Faith; and therefore thou hast little reason, O young man, to plead this example, to keep Christ, and thy soul asunder, who art every day under the call, the intreaties and wooings of Christ. But

Fifthly and lastly, I answer, The circumstances of time, and place, are rightly to bee considered; Now when Christ was triumphing on the Cross over sin, Satan, and the world, when he had made the devils a publick spectacle of scorn and derision, when hee was taking his leave of the world, and entring into his glory; Now hee puts a pardon into the Theefs hand,

hand, and crouds other favours and kindnesses upon him.

As in the *Roman* Triumphs, the Victor being ascended up to the Capitol in a Chariot of state, used to cast certain peeces of coyn among the people for them to pick up, which hee used not to do at other times: So our Lord Jesus Christ, in the day of his Triumph, and solemn Inauguration into his heavenly Kingdome, scatters some heavenly Jewels, that this Theef might pick up; which hee doth not, nor will not do every day; Or as in these daies it is usual with Princes to save some notorious malefactors at their coronation, when they enter upon their Kingdomes in triumph, which they do not use to do afterwards; So did Jesus Christ carry it toward this Theef; but this is not his ordinary way of saving and bringing souls to glory; and therefore do not, O young man! let not the Theefs late conversion, prove

a

a temptation, or an occasion of thy delaying thy repentance, and trifling away the prime-rose of thy daies in vanity and folly. And thus much may suffice to have spoken, by way of answer to the young mans Objections. I shall now speak a few words to old men, and so close up. Now

CHAP. IX.

IS it so commendable, so desirable, and so necessary for young men to bee good betimes, to seek and serve the Lord in the spring and morning of their youth, as hath been sufficiently demonstrated in this Treatise? Oh then that I could so wooe aged persons, as to win them (who yet have put off this great work) to seek and serve the Lord, before their glass be out, their sun set, and their souls lost for ever.

Oh that that Counsel of the Prophet might take hold upon your hearts, *Give glory to the Lord your God,*

Jer. 13. 16

God, before hee cause Darkness, and before your feet stumble (through age) upon the dark mountains; and while yee look for light, hee turn it into the shadow of death, and make it gross darkness.

I, but aged sinners may reply, *Is there any hope, any help for us?* is there any probability? is there any possibility, that ever such as wee are should return and finde mercy and favour with the Lord? wee who have lived so long without him, wee that have sinned so much against him, we that to this day are strangers to him, yea in arms against him: Is there any hope that wee white-headed sinners, who have withstood so many thousand offers of grace, and so many thousand motions of the Spirit, and so many thousand checks of conscience, and so many thousand tenders of Christ, and heaven, that ever we should obtain mercy, that ever wee should have our old hearts turned, our millions of sins pardoned, our vile na-

natures changed, and poor souls saved, &c.

I answer, That there is hope even for such as you are; all the Angels in Heaven, and all the men on Earth, cannot tell, but that you, even you, may obtain mercy and favour, that your souls dye not; with the Lord nothing is impossible, and for the grace of the Gospel, nothing is too hard: Now this I shall make evident by an induction of particulars. Thus

First, All were not called nor sent to work in the Vine-yard, at the first hour, some were called at the third hour, others, at the sixth, others, at the ninth, and some at the eleventh. God hath his several times of calling souls to himself: the eleventh hour was about five in the afternoon, an hour before Sun-set, when it was even time to leave work; and yet at this hour some were called, imployed and rewarded with the rest.

Mat. 20. 1. --17. The Roman penny was seven pence half penny.

Some

Doubts Resolved.

Some of the Fathers by the several hours mentioned in this parable, do understand the several ages of man; *viz.* childhood, youth, middle-age, and old-age, wherein poor souls are called and converted to Christ; the scope of the Parable, is, to signifie the free-grace of God in the calling of some in the spring and morning of their daies, and in the calling of others in their old-age, in the evening of their daies. But

Secondly, *Abraham* in the Old Testament, and *Nicodemus* in the New, were called and converted in their old-age, when there were but a few steps between them and the grave, between them and eternity.

Gen. 12.4
Joh. 3. 1,2,
3,4.c. 7. 50

I have read of one *Caius Nearius Victorius*, who was an old man three hundred years after the Apostles time, and had been a Pagan all his daies, and in his old-age, hee enquired and hearkened after Christ, and said hee would bee a Christian, an, *Simplicianus* hearing him say so, would not beleeve him, but when the Church saw a work of grace indeed upon him, there was shouting and dancing for gladness, and Psalms were sung in every Church, *Caius Marius Victorius* is become a Christian; And this was written for a wonder, that hee in his old age, and in his gray-hairs, should become a gracious Christian.

Aretius also speaks of a certain man in his time; It is no feigned story, saith hee, for I saw the man with my own eyes, hee was one that had been a most vile and desperate sinner, a drunkard, a swearer, a wanton, a gamester, and so hee continued to his Grayhairs; but at last it pleased God to set his sins in order before him, and the man was so troubled in conscience, that hee threw himself down upon the ground, calling unto Satan to take him away, provoking Satan to take him away; Devil, take thy own

Doubts Resolved. 253

own, Devil take thy own, I am thy own, take thy own: whereupon (saith *Aretius*) prayer was made for him; Christians prayed, they fasted and prayed, they prayed night and day; and it pleased God at last, that this poor aged sinner revived, converted to God, lived a godly life afterwards, and dyed comfortably.

Therefore let not the gray-headed sinner despair, though his spring be past, his summer overpast, and hee arrived at the fall of the leaf. But.

Thirdly, Divine Promises shall bee made good to returning souls, to repenting souls, to beleeving souls, bee they young or old, 2 Chron. 30. 9. *The Lord your God is gracious and merciful, and will not turn away his face from you, if you return unto him*, Joel 2. 13. *And rent your heart, and not your Garments, and turn unto the Lord your God: for hee is gracious and merciful, slow to anger,*

Isa. 1.18.
Jer. 3. 12
Isa. 43.22,
23,24,'25.
ch. 57.17,
18
Jer. 51. 5
John 3.16
Mark. 16.
16.

A a

ger, and of great kindness, and repenteth him of the evil, Isa. 55. 7. *Let the wicked forsake his way, and the unrighteous man his thoughts, and let him return unto the Lord, and hee will have mercy upon him, and to our God, for hee will abundantly pardon*: or hee will multiply to pardon. More of this you may see by reading of the Scriptures in the margent: all sorts of sinne shall bee pardoned to all sorts of beleeving and repenting sinners.

The new *Jerusalem* hath twelve Gates, to shew that there is every way access for all sorts and ranks of sinners, to come to Christ. Hee was born in an Inn, to shew that hee receives all comers, Young and Old, Poor and Rich, &c. But

Fourthly, The Lord hath declared by Oath, a greater delight in the conversion and salvation of poor sinners (whether they are young or old) than in the destruction and damnation of such, *Ezek.*

Ezek. 33. 11. *As I live, saith the Lord God, I have no pleasure in the death of the wicked, but that the wicked turn from his way and live:* Turn yee, turn yee, from your evil waies? for why wil yee dye? O yee house of *Israel*! Two things make a thing more credible.

1 The quality or dignity of the person speaking.

2 The manner of the speech: Now here you have the great God, not onely speaking, promising, but solemnly swearing that hee had rather poor sinners should live, than dye, bee happy, than miserable; therefore despair not, O aged sinner! but return unto the Lord, and thou shalt bee happy for ever. But

Fifthly, There is virtue enough in the precious blood of Jesus Christ, to wash and cleanse away all sin; not onely to cleanse away the young mans sins, but also to cleanse away the old mans sins: not onely to cleanse a sinner of

una guttula plus valet, quam cœlum & terra. Luther. One little drop is more worth than heaven and earth.

twenty years old, but to cleanse a sinner of fifty, sixty, yea, a hundred years old, 1 *John* 1. 7. *The blood of Jesus Christ his Son cleanseth us from all sin*, not simply from sin, but from all sin; there is such a power and efficacy in the blood of Christ, as is sufficient to cleanse all sorts of sinners, from all sorts of sins; there is virtue in the blood of the Lamb to wash out all the spots that are in the oldest sinners hearts; and therefore let not old sinners despair, let not them say, there is no hope, there is no help, as long as this fountain, the blood of Jesus Christ is open, for all sorts of sinners to wash in. But

Sixthly, The call and invitations of Christ in the Gospel, are general and indefinite, excluding no sort of sinners, *Rev.* 3. 20. *Behold, I stand at the door, and knock; if any man* (mark the indefiniteness of personal admittance) *hear my voice, and open the door, I will come in to him, and will*

Doubts Resolved.

will sup with him, and hee with mee; let the sinner bee old or young; a green head, or a gray head, if hee will but open the door, Christ will come in, and have communion and fellowship with him. So in that, *Mat.* 11. 28. turn to these Scriptures, and dwell upon them, they all clearly evidence the call and gracious invitations of Christ to bee to all sinners, to every sinner, hee excepts not a man, no, though never so old, nothing shall hinder the sinner, any sinner, the worst and most aged sinner from obtaining mercy, if hee bee willing to open to Christ, and to receive him as his Lord and King, *John* 6. 37. But

Seventhly, Christs pathetical lamentation over all sorts and ranks of sinners, declares his willingness to shew mercy to them; *O Jerusalem, Jerusalem,* (saith Christ, weeping over it) *that thou hadst known in this thy day, the things that belong to thy peace, &c. O that my people had hearkened unto mee!*

Isa. 55.1
John 7.37
Rev. 22.17

Luke 19. 41, 42
Psa. 81.13

Aa 2

mee! Christ weeps over *Jerusalem*, so did *Titus*, and so did *Marcellus* over *Syracuse*, and so did *Scipio* over *Carthage*; but they shed tears for them, whose blood they were to shed; but Christ weeps over the necks of those young and old sinners, who were to shed his blood. As a tender-hearted Father weeps over his rebellious children, when neither smiles, nor frowns, neither counsels, nor intreaties, will win them, or turn them from their evil waies. So doth Jesus Christ over these rebellious Jews upon whom nothing would work. But

Eightly and lastly, Though aged sinners have given Christ many thousand denials, yet hee hath not taken them, but after all, and in the face of all denials, hee still re-inforces his suit, and continues to beseech them by his Spirit, by his word, by his wounds, by his blood, by his messengers, and by his rebukes, to turn home to him, to embrace him, to beleeve in

Psa. 65. 1, 2
Rom. 10. 21

1 Joh. 5. 2, 3

in him, and to watch with him, that they may bee saved eternally by him; all which bespeaks gray-headed sinners, not to despair, nor to dispute, but to repent, return, and beleeve, that it may go well with them for ever. Consider seriously what hath been spoken, and the Lord make you wise for eternity.

FINIS.

Reader add as follows, pag. 120. l. 12. next to those words, nor seek the Lord to day.

I have read of a certain young man, who being admonished of the evil of his way and course, and pressed to leave his wickedness by the consideration of death, judgement, and eternity that was a coming, hee answered, what do you tell mee of these things, I will do well enough, for when death comes, I will speak but three words, and will help all; and so still he went on in his sinful waies, but in the end, coming to a bridge on horse-back, to go over a deep water, the horse stumbling, and hee labouring to recover his horse, but could not, at last hee let go the bridle, and gave up himself and horse to the waters, and was heard to say these three words, Devil take all. Here was three dreadful words indeed, and an example (with a witness) for all young men to beware, who think to repent with a three-word repentance at last.

Diabolus capiat omnia.

Lightning Source UK Ltd.
Milton Keynes UK
UKOW05f1831291015

261700UK00005B/84/P